UNLOCKING THE POWER
OF FATHERHOOD

UNLOCKING
THE POWER OF
FATHERHOOD

Glenn

Thank you for your
service to our great
state. Enjoy the
message

Gary D. Rogers

GARY D. ROGERS

Palmetto Publishing Group
Charleston, SC

Unlocking the Power of Fatherhood
Copyright © 2019 by Gary D. Rogers
All rights reserved

First Edition

Printed in the United States

ISBN-13: 978-1-64111-267-3
ISBN-10: 1-64111-267-0

TABLE OF CONTENTS

INTRODUCTION

This book is the story of a remarkable man and his family; of a man who overcame disabling disease as a child, plunged headlong into life's journey, and in the process shaped his life on his own terms. He took all that life had to throw at him, accepted every challenge and gave back more than he received. His journey demonstrates to us how we, too, can find happiness and contentment—even when life treats us unfairly and places a disproportionate share of challenges in our way.

Our world today can be a difficult place. Life can be complicated and confusing, and sometimes just plain unfair. Often when we find ourselves in a difficult place where we don't have any good options, we just don't seem to know what to do. As you read this story, you will discover that its characters found themselves more than once in just such a place. They found a path through the impossible, however, and they did it in ways that speak volumes to us today. The principles that guided them are like a lighthouse that shows the way through the storm. You, too, can navigate life's troubled waters by the light from that same lighthouse.

The members of the family that lived this story were just normal people like you and me, people who found ways to overcome whatever obstacle lay before them. It was a family that knew that in life there are some things that cannot be avoided, only confronted. They walked through their greatest challenge because the alternative was simply un-thinkable, and they refused to accept it. Their ways teach us that there are critical moments when the only viable option is to press through. Their ways teach us something equally important.

The road they chose demonstrates the value of the unencumbered power of fatherhood. In the pages that follow we will discuss the critical role of authentic masculinity. We will learn of the benefits our culture derives when men step into their purpose and attain to the best quali-ties that true manhood requires—men of honor, men of integrity, men driven to protect, men who stand for right regardless of the cost. We will learn of the unique value of these beings when the heart of a father overlays the strength of a man to make this a better place to live. This book is a call to arms for men to step forward and provide a safe haven that is only created when they demonstrate by word and deed that they are, indeed, good men.

You will find reassurance here. You will discover a way to enjoy the best of life regardless of what challenges are thrown at you. We are all fellow travelers on the same journey. We all have obstacles to face. We all make mistakes and we all are treated poorly at times—very poorly sometimes. The key to happiness is in how we choose to walk through the hard times. We cannot change the past, nor can we change the circumstances that are thrust upon us. All we can change is how we respond to them, and how we move forward.

For the incredible women out there, I want you to know that al-though there is a lot in this book addressed to men, much of what is here is meant for you, as well. The principles of life, the pursuit of purpose, the qualities that reside in a person of influence, they all ap-ply equally to women. I have taken time to challenge men to be men because that is my message and I am a man myself. I want women to know that your contributions are essential, and we need you in the fore-front of battle. Our children need you and our nation needs you. We need you in every nook and cranny of the country. There is no place where you are disqualified. Pay attention to the mother in Chapter 1— now, that was a strong woman. None of what happened would have been possible without her. This book would have not been written without her. Never, ever, let anyone tell you there's something you can't do because you're a woman. You have what it takes. We need you by our side as equal partners. Without you, none of us is going to accomplish all that we were meant to achieve. Together, joined in perfect union, we can make this world a better place for everyone.

In the pages that follow, I have given examples of how to walk through the difficult seasons of life and come out the other end better for it. The lessons to be learned here will guide you to becoming the man or woman you were meant to be. When you find that person, I believe you are going to like whom you have found.

CHAPTER 1

SOVEREIGNTY OF CHOICE

Two roads diverged in a wood, and I—
I took the one less traveled by,
And that has made all the difference.[1]
— Robert Frost

Storm clouds were gathering in the night sky high over East Texas as a father and son set out across the lake, headed toward the open water near the dam. They were buffeted by wind and wave as their small, flat-bottom boat bounced across the lake. Each cherished this time, just as they had enjoyed countless hours spent together on the rivers and salt marshes of the Texas Coast. Neither of them knew that their time together would soon be cut short. Tragedy was headed their way...but not on this night. Tonight, was a night for them, and them alone.

However, this is far from the beginning of the tale. Our story really begins five decades earlier...

THE CHOICE IS MADE

It was the late 1920's in a small town on the Texas Gulf Coast. Storm clouds were blowing into the soul of a young family just as surely as if they had rolled up from the Gulf's tepid waters. Father and mother were faced with a new reality, one that would shift their family's culture and echo down through the generations. Their decisions in the coming days would be crucial, and their choices would mold their family.

As they stood in a hospital room, they knew there was something terribly wrong with their little boy, the youngest of their three children. They hoped for good news—but the stoic realism that was the hallmark of each one's character whispered otherwise. The doctor came and escorted them to a place where they could speak privately. He was a good man and he liked this young couple very much, as everyone did. He summoned all the compassion he could muster to deliver the news he knew he must deliver.

As the father and mother had suspected, the doctor brought bad news—*Poliomyelitis.* The news hit them like a searing pain in the gut, one of those things that brings parents to their knees. The tears came in a way only a parent can understand—*Oh no, it can't be.* Pain and dread were etched on their faces. The hopes and dreams they'd had for their small son had shattered with that single word—polio. In an instant, those dreams turned into unanswerable questions and unspeakable fears.

I can see them now, the father with his head hung low, tears streaming down his face—the mother with her arms folded across her chest, her right hand covering her mouth, her fingers patting her lips while tears glistening in her eyes. They paused, looked at each other, and took deep breaths to calm themselves. They couldn't fall apart now, their boy needed them too much for that.

What could be done? they asked. The doctor summoned all his strength to give them the news he could not avoid delivering—*Incurable.* The young parents struggled to compose themselves even as more tears came. From the searing pain in their hearts came the critical question, *Will he survive?*

The doctor assured them, "We are doing all we can. The disease will have to run its course." Now let me translate that for you. He is on his own—he will have to fight off this deadly virus with a compromised immune system that had already proven itself inadequate to the task.

The parents had heard of other children who had not survived this ghastly disease. Polio had swept across the nation in near epidemic proportions, and medical science seemed powerless to stop it. What would become of their boy? Was he destined to live in a machine that would breathe for him? Many victims were so confined. The idea shook the father and mother to the core.

Each encounter with doctors and nurses brought more bad news, or no news at all, forcing the beleaguered couple to wonder which was worse. As they faced an uncertain future, they found that their faith and each other, was all they had to sustain them. But there was one thing they knew beyond any doubt—they loved their child with all their hearts, and they were determined to see him through this tragedy. Their immense capacity to love made the pain in their hearts even more searing. But while their pain was great, their love was greater.

Finally, there was news that brought a glimmer of hope—his lungs had been spared the onslaught of the disease, which meant he could breathe for himself, independent of machines. Then more news—the disease had settled into his legs, the right leg seemed to be the worst.

Something then settled in their souls, fueled by their deep love for their son—a steely determination to face head-on whatever was to come. The resolve they had learned on the farms and baseball fields of Texas began to overcome their fear.

The child's father, a professional baseball pitcher, faced an opponent he knew he absolutely *must* defeat. He was unaccustomed to losing, and did not intend to start now. The competitive fire that burned within him fueled his inner strength. He had faced down batter after batter with his blazing fastball and an enticing changeup that left each of them wondering what on earth had just happened. This time, however his opponent was not a man, but an unseen virus attacking his youngest son. And the road he must travel to defeat this opponent was far longer and more difficult than the sixty feet, six inches of infield between the pitcher's mound and the batter's box.

One day he came home from work to find his wife in the kitchen making coffee. She looked at him and said, "We need to talk." They sat down at the kitchen table and she poured him a cup of coffee. She had been thinking, and a decision had to be made. I can see them now, sitting over coffee and discussing pros, cons, and likely outcomes. Should they even consider...? What would become of their boy? And what would people say? Did that really matter, though? It really didn't.

Together they made the critical choice, the choice to speak for their son when he could not speak for himself.

There was a core strength in the young mother that would see her through the many dark nights to come. Raised on a Texas cotton farm in the early twentieth century, she developed a strength of character that was born of the pragmatism that way of life required. Unlike her sisters who worked in the home with their mother, she went to the fields with her father. She drove the cotton wagons and cleared the fields of weeds, learning to work alongside her dad. And she learned something else. *To make do.* For there was no safety net or credit card to fall back on if the crop failed. They just had to accept reality and make any resources they had stretch to the next year. There was no point in wishing things were different. Some would call her hard-headed. But it went deeper than that. She had a deep-seated instinct to know what to do and how to set the proper course.

It was that same core of confidence that now told her they needed to make a decision before they went to see the doctor. Thankfully, the individual strengths of this couple formed the ideal team their son needed in his struggle.

There at the kitchen table, the mother and father made the critical choice. They chose to embark on a difficult journey for the best reason in the world—their youngest was in trouble and there was no one else to help him. It was not the easy choice, nor perhaps, the road most traveled by, but it was the only road their love would let them take. In this critical moment the full power of fatherhood was unleashed.

The next day, they went to the hospital to meet with the doctor. The doctor came with more bad news. Their son would never live a normal life like other children. He would never crawl or walk, never ride a bicycle, climb a ladder, or drive a car. "We need to put braces on his legs", he said.

This time, the news did not bring them to their knees, for the boy's father had an incredible woman beside him. This time, she was not sitting in the stands cheering him on as he faced down the best the other team had to send against him. This time they stood shoulder to shoulder. He knew that he could depend on her deep well of wisdom and good judgement when it came time to make a decision. They stood together in perfect union, determined to see their son live the life he was born to live. They paused, took deep breaths, and looked at each other one last time to reaffirm their decision. Finally, with one united, creative voice, they turned to the doctor and said, "No. You are not putting braces on his legs. He will walk. He will live a normal life. We will see to it."

There it was—the critical act of sovereignty their boy so desperately needed.

In that critical moment in time, armed with the power of a simple two-letter word, they set their son's now-shaky feet on the path to fulfill all that was meant for him to accomplish, to set a course where he would achieve more than they could dare hope for. In one incredible moment, their decision changed everything. In that moment, they reclaimed the sovereignty over their son's future the disease had tried to steal.

It was just like one of the dad's fastballs with two outs and the bases loaded. One fastball high and tight on the inside corner, rocking the batter back on his heels. One simple *no* carried the day for their son, fighting for his life. Their boy was going to make it! Their son would have his life back. They would make sure of it.

Something more was in play here. Something no doctor could see, something no test could measure. Within their son beat the heart of a fighter. A boy who would grow into a man who did not quit, nor allow his sons to do so. He learned to crawl and eventually walk because his family rallied around him—mother, father, sister, brother. Watching and fighting for their boy, their Billy Ray.

With an unwavering drive, incredibly good nature, and infectious smile on his face, Billy Ray charged headlong into life. He did it with a limp, with one good leg and the other he called his "bum leg." He did it with a compromised immune system that would fail him again, and with finality much too early in life. He took all this world had to give, and gave back more than he got. Nothing was ever started that he didn't finish; no obstacle was ever met with "I can't." He reveled in the challenge of doing things that seemed beyond his reach, things "they" said could not be done.

Billy Ray didn't have two good legs like his friends. But he did have something just as valuable—his home was a place where the culture of fatherhood had been established in love and determination. His strength and resiliency were drawn from two incredible people who stood together and spoke for him when he could not speak for himself. His roots sank deep into the two who had given him life. He drew sustenance from them and developed a strength of character and determination of will that sustained him as he overcame great physical limitation.

The remarkable thing is this—his family acted like it was all so normal.

SUPREMACY OVER CIRCUMSTANCE

It seemed normal because his family treated his condition as normal. Obstacles in life are a normal part of the human condition. The parents dealt with their son's health as it was, not how they wanted it to be. They accepted his condition and were determined to see him triumph over it.

We all face the same choice. Trying to deal with life as you wish it were, rather than what it actually is, will lead to a life held captive to circumstance. Dealing with things as they are leads to a life well-lived. Billy Ray's parents did not smother him with debilitating sympathy or try to make things easy for him. They never let him quit, and they never let him feel sorry for himself. In the end, he became the most incredible man that I have ever known.

The one thing Billy Ray never did was ask *why* this had happened to him. When the critically difficult times come to you, asking the *why* question can undermine you and turn you into a victim. Focusing on why this is happening to you—something you could never hope to truly answer, anyway—can be debilitating and mire you in the muck of self-pity. Self-pity is a strangling weed that will grow and eventually take control. I know this, because I made the *why* mistake, and it turned out very badly.

For a period of twelve years I ran a home building business—just before the crash in 2008. The housing market had already begun to soften ahead of that. I had built some spec homes that were not selling, pre-orders were drying up, and finances were getting tight—our resources were dwindling and creditors were calling. I began to wonder why this was happening to me. In my mind, I listed all the reasons why this shouldn't be happening: I was a good guy, I treated my customers well, I helped people, I was a man of integrity. And then came a fateful day when I cracked. I crossed a line and verbalized my despair. I cried out, "Why is this happening to me? It's just not fair."

After that, my *It's not fair* complaint became the subject of far too many conversations. It became my story. I was doing the very thing my dad had taught me not to do. I believe that my negative outlook only made matters worse. I turned away from the very thing that my father had modeled for me. I turned my heart to becoming a victim.

As long as I complained about the unfairness of my situation, I prolonged the misery of it all. As this continued, I sank deeper and deeper into despair, until the muck of self-pity almost suffocated me. I was immobilized, stuck and utterly miserable, and miserable to be around. It was only when I turned back to my roots and accepted life as it was that things began to turn around.

Asking something of life puts your circumstances in the driver seat. The thing is, when trouble comes, you don't have spare energy or resources to spend time on feeling sorry for yourself or complaining about the unfairness of your situation. At that critical juncture, you need to be on point, focused like a soldier leading his infantry company through the battle field. Like him, you must stay vigilant or be destroyed. Life never promises us "fair." Staying in the present, accepting the challenges in our path, and pressing through to our purpose is the only thing that will see you through.

The boy in that hospital bed grew into a man who doggedly rejected the concept that life owed him something. Although he had been afflicted by polio, he refused to become a victim. Guided by his parents, his fighter's heart rejected out of hand the temptation to descend into self-pity. He asked nothing from life, but set his own course and took personal responsibility to make the most of the life he had.

Who was this boy, you may ask? I've already told you his given name was Billy Ray. The woman he loved called him Bill. My brother and I had the distinct privilege and indescribable honor of calling him Dad. Every day of our youth, my brother and I were taught a lesson in courage and character. I do not remember seeing my father go to bed, nor do I remember seeing him get up. I do, however, remember seeing him come home, day after day, exhausted from work, one leg doing the work of two. There was never a complaint. Things were just as they were.

There were no grand speeches, just a life well-lived that taught us what it was to be men and taught us to be fathers. In the early days of the twentieth century, they referred to someone like my dad as a cripple and wrote off his chances at a normal life. Today, they would offer him a handicap card for his car. His response would still be the same, "No thanks, save it for someone who needs it." Interestingly, when my wife first met him she had no idea that he had a *bum leg*. He was a pretty convincing fellow because *he* was convinced. He did not see himself as a handicapped person.

YOUR AUTHORITY TO REIGN AS SOVEREIGN

In the coming pages, you will hear more stories about this incredible man, the lessons taught by the way he lived, and the care he had for others. You will learn what it is to be a real man, how to chart your own course and claim sovereignty over your life. I began this work motivated to honor this man, and perhaps help fill father-shaped holes in the souls of those less fortunate than my brother and me. But my intent has grown into something more, a desire to share what I know of what it takes to stare down the most difficult of life's challenges and walk through them as true women and men.

Perhaps you were not as fortunate as I to have a model to follow. Maybe your back is against the wall and you have one, and only one, critical move facing you. You know what I'm talking about—one of those life-altering decisions. Maybe you have a child in crisis and you are his only option. Or maybe you, as I, are deeply concerned for our country's direction and what we are bequeathing the coming generations.

Likely, the question in your heart is: "How can I know what to do?"

The answer is found in the principles stored deep in your soul. The courage is found in your character. The solution is never found in walking away or taking the easy way out. The answer is found in the sovereignty of choice. Like the "No" that a young father and mother delivered to a doctor ninety years ago that saved their son's life. They didn't have a plan. They just knew they were going to see their boy walk. *They were determined to see to it.*

The same strength they tapped into resides in you. It comes from an endowment established by your Creator. One of those things Thomas Jefferson and his fellow framers wrote about in the summer of 1776.

You may be a father who was not as privileged as I to have such a good model to follow. You may be a single mom struggling to raise your children on your own. You may be the child who did not have a father in your life. You may be one of many who have a father-shaped hole in your soul. If that is so, I hope the concepts in this book will help to fill it. Perhaps one of the many incredible fathers we have in this country will come along and lend a hand. Perhaps one of the incredibly gifted moms who have walked the road you are traveling will come along and impart that single nugget of wisdom you so desperately need.

In the absence of all of that, know this. You can do it. You have everything you need within you, it is written in your DNA—no one can take it from you.

If you learn to apply the principles laid out in this book, you, too, can learn to walk through the storms of life and emerge victorious. You may have to do it with one "bum leg", but *you can do it.* You can lead your children to do the same, raise them to be men and women of character, integrity, and honor. You can be the catalyst of change that alters the course of our nation.

If you accept the challenge, maybe, just maybe, we can change a generation and redeem a nation. Fatherhood is much more than molding and rescuing children. It is also about building a culture in which a nation can excel. Fatherhood is about men stepping up to be men, determined to sustain a nation where *all* people have the opportunity to live life to its fullest. It is about women and men leading us to a place where we respect each of life's fellow travelers, even though they may hold beliefs that are counter to those we ourselves hold most dear.

Know this one thing for certain—you have authority. There is a place, the place of your purpose, where you are endowed with the power to choose, empowered to claim your sovereign right of choice. Like the choice made so many years ago that saved my dad, you, too, have the power to reign, to claim your place of sovereignty.

Nothing disqualifies you. The things that happened to you in the past, the family situation you came from, and the mistakes you have made, only serve to give you the understanding you need to live the life for which you were truly designed. Just as it was with that amazing man and his "bum leg." Each day is made up of hundreds of choices—to go right or left, forward or backward, right or wrong, truth or deceit, courage or fear. The sum of these choices is what makes us who we are. The reality is, the right choice made today makes the right choice easier tomorrow.

Billy Ray lived his life in such a way that choosing well became automatic, something he did without thinking. With every choice he made to turn and confront his obstacles, he was writing his story, and what an amazing story it was. His was a story built on choosing to tackle every challenge that came at him.

The question before you is this—what is the story *you* are going to write? Will it be the story you were born to write? Like all choices, it's yours to make.

Let's face it—there are times when you have no good choices. Your choices are to stay in the frying pan or jump out into the fire. I'm sorry, but that is just the way life is. There are times when we grow weary of being knocked down and getting up only to be knocked down again. I understand because that was the way I felt as my business was failing. I'm sure that was the way my dad felt as a child when he tried over and over to learn to walk. We can come to a place where circumstances overwhelm, appearing to take away our birthright, and we are just plain exhausted.

But there is one thing that life cannot take away from you—your power to choose to press on until you gain the ultimate victory. It is the power to look circumstance in the face and say *No, you are not putting braces on my destiny.* Your will to keep going is your sovereign right. If you persevere you can win and write the story you were meant to write—the unique story of you.

The choice that is the foundation of everything is this: Who is going to reign over your life?

Your life is yours, and that means *you* own it. You only have one of them. There is not much we can do to control our circumstances or what others do to us. Just as that child in the hospital had no choice whether he had polio or not. He did, however, have many life-defining choices ahead of him, choices that belonged to him. In different ways, we all face the same intensity of challenge he faced. Everyone has the same opportunity to choose greatness. Everyone has the capacity to rule over their life.

There are times when life challenges us and tests our character beyond what we think we can endure. Those times define us and set the course of our life. Saying "No" to the easy choice in these critical times takes courage but yields great reward. If we choose well and persevere, our feet will land on the road that leads us to our destiny, and we will have earned the right to be called fathers. If we choose well, we claim our right to exert sovereignty over our own lives.

Everyone has the capacity to choose greatness.

CHAPTER 1 REVIEW QUESTIONS

1. Define sovereignty. What are the powers of a sovereign?

2. Contrast these two opposing life positions: One man tries to deal with life as they wish it were right now. One man embraces the realities of life as they are right now.

3. How would the concept of choice as demonstrated by the young mother and father empower you to live our own life to the fullest? Think of specific examples.

4. What is the value of saying "No" to the easy choice? What are the critical choices that you are facing today?

5. Can you think of examples in your life where you have made a good choice and that made making a good choice easier in the future? What about the other side, i.e. bad choices?

6. Think about the concept of taking personal responsibility for your life. How can this principle help you confront the inherent unfairness that life imposes on us?

CHAPTER 2

DARK NIGHT ON STRIKER CREEK

Whoever is careless with the truth in small matters
cannot be trusted with important matters.[2]
— Albert Einstein

In the old west there was a saying that went like this: *A man is as good as his word.* It meant the quality of a person could be measured by his or her commitment to always telling the truth. Understood on a deeper level, it meant he may be wrong, or she may not understand, but every word from his or her mouth was a statement which represented what they believed to be true. It also meant that when a man made an agreement he was going to follow through on what he said, and would abide by not only the agreement he had made, but also the intent of the agreement.

This level of truthfulness is essential to the maintenance of an orderly society. Our system of justice, for example, depends on the truthfulness of our witnesses. Likewise, our system of commerce depends on people fulfilling their commitments in their business transactions. When they don't, things end up in court and everyone loses. A high level of integrity means a person is committed to doing what they said they would, simply because they said so.

I understand that this is a high standard, and we as people often fall short. However, the diligent pursuit of truthfulness and accountability makes us trustworthy and contributes to a healthy self-image, leading to contentment and meaningful personal relationships. When a person is known to be trustworthy, people will give him the benefit of the doubt when he makes a mistake or is wrong. That is the mark of healthy relationships.

ESSENTIAL NATURE OF TRUTH

Truth represents that which sustains and nourishes, the place where our roots sink deep, where justice is maintained, and whence our character derives its resiliency. Truth is where we find direction to weather the storms of life and make the most difficult of life's decisions. Truth defines that which is right and that which is wrong. Truth creates stability and nourishes growth and creativity. Thus, truth forms the essential ethic through which civilization flourishes and we find security.

However, a wise people are compelled to honestly evaluate what they believe, in order to assure it is right. For us to grow, we must be willing to admit when we are wrong and change our positions when necessary. The capability of a man to simply say, "I was wrong, will you please forgive me?" is a sign of true masculinity.

Self-evaluation is the evolutionary process by which we grow in understanding and in the fairness with which we treat our fellow travelers in life. There was a time when it was thought that girls were not as good as boys in math, and that people of color were not very intelligent. I would encourage you to watch the movie Hidden Figures.[3] It's the story of three extremely capable black women who worked in the space program. In it you will see their struggle to break through the stereotypes of the day, and the incredible contribution they made. Without the extraordinarily complex math, computer, and engineering skills they performed, we would not have sent our astronauts into orbit.

In my experience, some of the best mathematicians I've known have been women, and skin color had nothing to do with their capability.

Truth is a foundational pillar of the culture of fatherhood. A child's safety is derived from truth, and in its embrace they grow into adulthood. Truth is the place where their confidence is formed, and where they gain the courage to meet life's challenges straight on. Children must have a stable foundation of truth upon which to build their self-confidence. They need to know that their foundation is not subject to the whims of circumstance. It is the place where men become men and women become women. These are not distinctions awarded through age, but rather are earned positions derived from our devotion to the fundamental principles of right and wrong.

IT WAS A DARK AND STORMY NIGHT….IN 1975.

I was working on my master's degree in aquatic ecology and had been assigned the task of establishing two sampling locations on my thesis lake, Striker Creek Reservoir. I was to take a series of water samples during the day and again at night, starting at the surface and proceeding down through the water column to the bottom. It was essential that the boat remain stationary during the sampling so the samples would be taken from a fixed place. One location was in the open water near the dam. The second was among the flooded timber at the upper end of the reservoir.

My parents were coming to visit my new bride and me. It was my chance to show my dad what I was working on, and I wanted him to be proud of me. I was excited to share the time with my dad, as he was with me.

As we launched the boat that night, the wind was strong and the waves were high. Growing up on the Texas Gulf Coast, we had been on rough water together countless times. As the light, flat-bottomed boat bounced across the lake, we were jarred repeatedly. He looked at me and shouted above the wind, "If this is what I get for taking you out on the water all your life, well I guess I deserve it!" He then gave me the endearing grin that I loved so well. Even though he struggled to maintain balance with only one good leg, the smile never left his face. Because he was with one of his boys--the thing he loved most.

It was a dark night, father and son were buffeted by wind and wave, but cherished this time together, as we had so many times before. Little did we know that we had precious little time left to spend together.

We pulled up to the open water sampling location. We were centered between a lighted boat dock on one side and a power station on the other. I threw the anchor overboard and began collecting samples.

It was then I noticed we were moving. The wind was pushing us, dragging the anchor. The anchor was not strong enough to hold against the storm, yet the boat needed to be stationary for the sampling to be accurate. I asked my father what he thought I should do, a very natural question to ask. He always knew how to help me make a good decision. Together, we decided to take the samples anyway. We finished, pulled up the anchor, and headed up the lake toward the flooded timber. Again, the wind and waves made it a very rough ride. We laughed as we went. I threw the throttle wide open to make the journey more interesting, and he just laughed.

We found the huge, dead oak tree that I had marked earlier in the day, and tied off to it with the anchor rope. The boat was again pushed by the wind. The rope pulled tight, but the tree held. Somehow, the dead oak was still strong, and its roots still anchored deep in the soil beneath the lake. The tree was unmovable in the storm. It still stood where its seed had fallen many years before the reservoir had flooded, where it had grown from a sapling, drawing sustenance from that same soil. So, this time, my samples were taken from a single place because the tree had grown sturdy and flourished there.

There in the boat with me was the man who, just as that oak tree, represented a single, reliable standard. When I would go to him and ask for advice, I usually walked away thinking, "Yes, I thought that was what he would tell me." His wisdom held the truth I already knew deep down somewhere, even if it wasn't what I particularly wanted to hear at that moment. My character was formed from my roots which had sunk deep into him, nourishing me with his wisdom. He had done his job well, he had given me everything I needed to become who I was meant to be.

Although his time among us was growing short, on that night in the storm, I was unafraid of the dark, the wind, or the waves. I was safe and secure because he was there with me. It was security gleaned from a knowledge that I always knew where he stood, and where I could find him.

Such is the essence of true manhood.

THE INDISPENSABLE ROLE OF A FATHER

In the years since that stormy night, I have weathered difficult times, always drawing sustenance from the man who had been in the boat with me. His unwavering character lived on in my heart long after he was gone. Billy Ray remained my standard against which all my decisions were measured. With him, there was right and there was wrong. That which was true yesterday was true today. He always stood for the right, no matter what it cost him. This quality defined him as a man of character and garnered the respect of all who knew him.

To me he was a tree, not an anchor. He was unmovable, an unchangeable standard. On those difficult nights in my home office as my business was crumbling and I was faced with difficult decisions, I could always find one of his principles to guide me. The consequences of decisions made were not always pleasant, but the decision was the right one to make. In the aftermath of those choices, I could always take solace in the person I had become.

It is because of his guidance that I have come to like who I am as a man. And when my difficult decisions are based on his tested principles, things invariably turn out well.

Billy Ray was joined in life by a remarkable woman who saw through his limp and what he called his "bum leg." She saw a man who knew what it was to be a man—someone on whom she could depend. Someone worthy, in whom to invest her tremendous capacity to love. Together they created the culture of fatherhood in our home for my brother and me. We knew what was proper and courteous, and what was not. We learned how to treat people well through the evidence of how we ourselves were treated. We learned the value of correction in an atmosphere of love. We were never shocked or had the rug pulled out from under us. Things were predictable, and the high standards never changed. It was a remarkable upbringing. I understand how incredibly blessed I am to have had such a home as this, even though my time with my father was too short. I wish everyone was blessed to have such a good model to follow, but I know it is not so. That understanding is the impetus for writing this book. I believe that regardless of our backgrounds, we all have the ability to choose the standard of truth as a guiding principle of our lives.

For the first twenty-seven years of my life, I saw firsthand what it was to be a man. My father's purpose was to teach me how to think and how to weigh decisions against standards and truth. As I grew older, I learned to make good decisions through the challenging conversations he initiated. By this process, he taught me to think like a man of character and ultimately choose what was right. He questioned me using concepts that were very natural for him. Concepts like:

- If it were you, would you want to be treated that way?
- Is that the kind of person you want to be?
- Is that what you said you would do?

These were not rhetorical questions; he expected me to really think about and answer them. Then there was my personal favorite…or sometimes my least favorite:

- Can't never could do anything.

This is a concept that means that you will never overcome if you tell yourself that you are incapable of conquering life's difficult challenges. It is a powerful statement meant to establish the inner strength one needs to achieve their purpose.

The last one was far too difficult to ignore. Picture, if you will, a baby learning to walk. Stumbling into his parents' arms with a grin on his face and two good legs beneath him. Now picture my dad, his right leg with the muscles taken by polio, learning to use it as a crutch. Picture that baby and all the times he fell and then got up again. A boy who would never quit until he learned to walk. This was the way he tackled each of life's challenges. He would simply keep going no matter the hardship, and in the end, he would overcome.

Now try to imagine ignoring him when he says, Can't never could do anything. To him things were simple. Are you going to say, "I can't walk, I have a bum leg." Or, are you going to be the person who says, "I have one good leg; that's all I need."

My father taught us the value of responsibility and persistence, and at the time, it all seemed so beautifully normal.

Fathers teach, but more important, they *challenge* boys and girls to grow into men and women. He challenges them to conduct their lives measured against a high, reliable, fixed standard. Only then will they have the character and integrity to conquer life's storms. And in the process, they will find enough energy to help those who don't.

These will be the men and women who are dependable, doing the right thing no matter the cost—men and women of influence.

Throughout the generations, certain inalienable truths abide. They remain absolute and are not be subject to the whims of men or circumstance. Truths like equality, freedom, empathy, honesty, courage, mercy, bravery, selflessness, defending the vulnerable, respect for all life, and many more. Fatherhood is a primary keeper of these truths, and those fathers hold their children accountable to them.

When all is said and done, the most important truth of all is this: In the best of all worlds, there is always a place of love to be found in the arms of a father. Like truth, which is not subject to the whims of circumstance, so should be the love of a father.

Maybe your experience with your father has not been good—maybe it has been more like abuse than love. You may not have been fortunate to have a father whose arms were a place of love and safety. I understand if you can't relate to what I am saying. That doesn't mean you are disqualified from finding that relationship in another father, or from becoming a loving father yourself. In fact, many times when we go through painful experiences, we come out better equipped to understand what others are feeling. You may find that your bad experience turns you into the very person another wounded soul needs. If this is you, know that you are not damaged goods, and you have everything in you needed to rise above the past. You may have exactly the experience that someone else needs, the compassion to understand, and the will to be their safe place.

Your unique experiences may create a wisdom in you that qualifies you to be the father that some wounded soul longs for.

No matter what our individual experiences with fathers are, we can still be everything we were meant to be, we can still find the love we so desperately need, and we can live a life whose foundation is based on truth. Truth can be the place where we find safety and acquire an unquestioned commitment to becoming the best that we can be. If we choose wisely, we can look back on our lives and see that truth has led us through the tough times, directed us to the right decisions, and nurtured a spirit of compassion in us. In the end, if you choose the road less traveled, dedicated to a life of integrity, you will be able to look at yourself in the mirror and like the person that you see.

CHAPTER 2 REVIEW QUESTIONS

1. What are the basic truths that define or motivate you?
2. Contrast the written letter of an agreement with the intent of those making the agreement. What are your responsibilities in each area?
3. What does the adherence to the truth say about the quality of a person?
4. How does the simple statement, "I was wrong, will you please forgive me?" improve personal relationships? What does it say about a man who is willing to express it?
5. On a very personal level, how would an immovable foundation of truth strengthen you and sustain you through life's storms?
6. If you examine yourself, where do you see that your standards of truth need to be strengthened?
7. What two personal qualities are formed by a dedication to an immovable standard of truthfulness?
8. Construct a plan to shore up your personal standards of truth. What are the specific actions you want to take to implement your plan?

CHAPTER 3

STANDARDS

Is the beam from a lighthouse affected by howling wind and rain? It remains
perfectly steadfast and unaffected by the storm. Your true self is like that.
Nothing can ever harm you once you are consciously aware that it is so.[4]
— *Vernon Howard*

In this present time when things are in a constant state of change
and instability, do you find yourself looking for something that is
anchored, like that old tree in Striker Creek Reservoir?

Do you ever long for a day when you can count on a person, place,
or thing to simply stay in one place so there is some stability in your life?
Do you grow weary of waking each day and turning on the news only
to be faced with the latest catastrophic problem that signals the end of
the republic? And then getting up the next morning only to find that it
was not that big a deal and has been replaced by another catastrophe
or a new evil villain. Is there so much instability that you are concerned
for what will become of our nation and the way of life that will be left
for our grandchildren?

The concern over unbridled change is very legitimate. Allowing
change to go too far without reasoned constraint carries with it a danger that we must guard against. However, embracing reliably vetted

change is vital because it is the way we grow and advance. It is the way we right the wrongs of the past and protect those who have been short-changed by society. Sometimes change gets messy, particularly when it gets into the political arena, but let me reassure you, we are going to be okay. Our country is strong, and we always find our way through to a better future.

However, that does not happen automatically; it only happens when we remain vigilant. We need to be aware that many great civilizations crumbled when they failed to remain diligent, and allowed their standards to degrade. If we fail in our vigilance to maintain integrity, we could easily go the same way.

ENLISTING STANDARDS TO MANAGE CHANGE

The question before us is this: How can we make the necessary changes while avoiding the creation of bigger problems?

That is called the law of unintended consequences, and we need to guard against it. This is where our standards become so incredibly vital, for they are what keeps us grounded. Guarding against the law of unintended consequences and assessing the wisdom of a change is the job of our standards.

A good example of the application of a high standard is the US Constitution. Our founding fathers knew it wasn't perfect, but they made it very difficult to change. A good example of how to view standards. Their good judgment in writing our constitution came from a deep well of wisdom.

How do we know what needs to be changed and what does not? Well, that decision takes judgment, wisdom, and experience. It takes a reasoned, objective mind that can look at the evidence and construct a solution that works.

The hallmark standards which will serve us well are Fidelity, Faithfulness, Loyalty, Responsibility, Courage, Commitment, Devotion to Service, and Dedication to Standing for the Right simply because it is right. The personal cost we may incur cannot be in the equation, not if we want to claim to be men. I've often thought that a man's ethics are only worth what he is willing to pay for them. There are critical times when true men need to take a stand and simply do the right thing, regardless of the personal cost.

That willingness is the essence of true masculinity, it is the engine of courage.

SELF-ASSURANCE DERIVED FROM IMMUTABLE CORE STANDARDS

The ability to rely on our inner belief systems rather than external influences is a stabilizing quality of the human spirit. A thoughtful person who knows what he believes and trusts his own judgment is a person who is equipped for success. This quality of self-reliance is essential in today's world where technology has put instant information into the hands of everyone. Social media has raised the power of peer pressure to unprecedented levels. This is particularly dangerous to our youth who are still in their formative years, trying to figure out who they are. We need to be cognizant of the fact that social media gives a platform to the bully, and that this is weighing heavily on the mental wellbeing of many in their adolescent years. It is such a problem that it has its own name—cyber-bullying. It has even cost the lives of too many of our children.

The importance of raising children to be secure in who they are and what they believe has thus never been more critical. Self-assurance is like the beam from a lighthouse that will show them the way back when the storms of life blow hard against them. The need for fathers today is more critical than ever before.

Let's start with an illustration—the Columbia River.[5] The area where the Columbia River flows into the Pacific Ocean is one of the most treacherous confluences in the world. Without a river delta to mitigate, the current of the Columbia River is focused "like a fire hose" pointing straight out into the Pacific. The Columbia Bar is an area of shifting sand bars and shoals where the river drops its sediment, often creating large standing waves. Ships entering or exiting the river must cross over the bar with its constantly changing conditions. Here, they can encounter 20 to 30-foot waves. Conditions can go from calm to life-threatening in a matter of minutes.

To aid sailors in this treacherous environment, The United States Coast Guard established the internationally respected National Motor Lifeboat School at Cape Disappointment, where they operate in some of the roughest waters in the world. The Columbia Bar has become known as the "Graveyard of the Pacific," where about 2000 large ships have sunk since 1792. A core of accomplished harbor pilots now guides ships safely across the bar.

Overlooking the bar are two lighthouses that pilots use as fixed points of navigation—Cape Disappointment Light, and North Head Lighthouse. Interesting things, lighthouses. They are big and heavy, and they don't move. When a harbor pilot brings a ship into the Columbia River and is fighting 30-foot waves that are pushing him around, a fixed-point reference to guide them is essential. Without it, they risk going down with yet another ship into that watery graveyard.

The lighthouse is a tangible symbol of a belief system that trusts its standards. Its beam of light illuminates the value of a standard's immutable nature.

Here is an interesting fact—both of the above lighthouses have already been replaced by modern technology with superior functions. The Coast Guard was planning on closing the Cape Disappointment Light but retained it after the harbor pilots opposed its closing. They held onto their lighthouse, because it was the one thing they could trust with their lives. They carried an ingrained belief that the lighthouse could always be trusted. The pilots knew that no matter how strong the wind, rain, or waves—or bad the technological glitches—the light from Cape Disappointment Light would not waver; it would show them the way home, the way to those they loved.

The concept of high standards is like the lighthouse that establishes a beacon illuminating that which is true, right, just, fair, and moral. Standards are the place where the seeds of our character are planted and where they are nourished. They represent the stable soil in which character is formed and grows until the day we are ready to stand and charge off in search of life's purpose.

Life's important decisions are best made when properly measured by one's code of standards. A life dedicated to a high moral standard is a life well lived. It is a life marked by self-respect. Moral standards lead us back to our roots when the storms of life push us off course. In those times when bad decisions take us to an unhealthy place, it is our standards that show us the way home. When a community or a nation loses its way, it is the people who have dedicated their lives to unshakable standards who must stand and show the nation the way back, even if sacrificing their own comfort or self-interest to do so. They are like the lighthouse on the coast that shows the ship's pilot the way into harbor. If you choose to, you can count yourself among their number. You have the capacity within you.

FINDING EMPOWERMENT AMID THE CHALLENGE

Who are these people who sacrifice themselves, and where are they found?

William F Halsey, the great American naval commander of World War II, may have said it best. "There are no great men; there are only great challenges that ordinary men are forced by circumstances to meet."[6] Halsey commanded a formidable aircraft carrier group and led a great many of the men into battle in the Pacific. Those men stood, endured the maelstrom, and rose to greatness.

Where do people find the courage and drive necessary to meet life's great challenges? What compelled the men and women of the New York City Fire and Police Departments to charge into the World Trade Center on September 11, 2001, when the buildings were ablaze? What caused the soldiers of the 82nd and 101st Airborne Divisions to jump into the night sky over Normandy on D Day?

Where did the men and women who marched to the bridge in Selma, Alabama, on that Sunday in March, 1965, find courage to do so and to face merciless beatings? Do you know why they did that? It was to get the right to vote. Into which deep part of their souls did they reach to give themselves that capability? Where did they find the fortitude to put themselves in harm's way and rescue or fight for complete strangers?

The place into which they reached was a sacred place deep inside them. It was a place where self-respect and devotion to duty were stored.

I grew up with a man who drew on years of practicing courage and character when times were tough. I know where he found it. He found it in the roots of a childhood that drove him to learn to walk when he had one good leg and one that wasn't. His parents had a choice to make for him. Were they going to count themselves with those who would let him make excuses? Or, were they going to instill in him the courage to make do with what he had and be thankful for it? The drive of these two re-markable people birthed the heart of a fighter within their son, enabling him to keep on trying even though it was hard and sometimes painful.

It is interesting that he never complained of being treated unfairly in life when his very physical condition was extraordinarily unfair. He avoid-ed the "it's not fair" trap because he knew it would destroy him. His core standard was a simple one—*I will take all that life throws at me, I will not stop until I have overcome, and I will give back better than I got.* He taught his sons that core standard, and it is the reason my brother and I are who we are today. Because of his positive mindset, rather than fighting discouragement, he actually got charged up every time he encountered a new challenge.

My dad had bought a boat several years earlier. We lived two blocks from a boat dock on the Old Brazos River Channel in Freeport, Texas. He had taught my brother and me to ski as well as numerous other friends and family. Then came the day when he did what we all expected him to do. The whole thing was not surprising, it was all kind of normal. This day was the day *he* decided to learn to ski. His best friend was enlisted to drive the boat. I stood on the bank watching with my mother. She was worried, but she knew better than to try to talk him out of it. It never worked, anyway.

Most skiers learn to ski by learning on two skis and then later advancing their skills to use just a single ski. In the process of learning to slalom, they always start by getting up on both skis. As we would say today, *Houston we have a problem.* Dad only had one good leg—he would have to learn on one ski.

Many would say it couldn't be done. He had heard those words before, and such naysaying always made him grin and only served to make him more determined. He was energized by the impossible. We watched him get up and fall repeatedly, until he was spent. My mother was convinced he would drown himself. Finally, exhausted, he stopped. They pulled up to the boat dock and I ran over, asking him what he was going to do. He looked at me, put his hand on my shoulder, and said, "Well, son, we'll come back tomorrow." There were no theatrics; it was the most natural thing in the world.

Tomorrow came, and with it he got up on his single ski. He skied and skied, having a great time. The interesting thing is, I don't remember him skiing many times after that. I just think he was proving once again that he could do what they said was impossible. He really enjoyed the challenge of overcoming that which could not be overcome. It all seemed so normal because he accepted what life had given him, and was thankful for it.

I don't know if normal is the right word, but I do know that every woman and every man has the same strength in them that enabled him to triumph over the odds. If you question whether I'm talking to you, I *am* talking to you.

Somewhere amid the challenges lay my father's empowerment, fueled by the moral code that had developed within him. It found its full expression in his love for his wife and two boys. Unfaithfulness had no place in his world. Responsibility and service fulfilled him. Everyone in town knew him, and knew his moral and ethical standards. His influence seemed universal among family and friends. As a boy and later a young man, I would occasionally find one of my surrogate fathers correcting me with the words, "Your dad wouldn't let you do that." Let's just say I appreciate that a lot more now than when I was a teenager. Over the years I learned how to trust what he had shown me and find security in his ways.

As a young man, I became accustomed to following the ways of my father, which did not win a plethora of popularity contests. In fact, those standards were misunderstood by many and ridiculed by others. Despite all that, now I awaken each day, examine myself in the mirror, and when I think of the times I was faithful to my true self, I like the person looking back at me.

The standards established in our home also shaped an environment where failure was acceptable. Quitting or avoiding difficulties were discouraged, mainly through the use of uncomfortably probing questions, because my father knew it was through the difficult paths that we would become men. Underlying it all was a clear understanding that his love had no limit.

I learned a great life lesson that day on the banks of the Brazos. I learned the power of setting one's mind on a goal and pursuing that goal with everything you have. I have come to recognize that goal-pursuit was my father's core value. It was how he learned to walk and how he fought his way to his purpose. This was the standard upon which all his other standards were founded.

All men and women who rise to greatness, I believe, draw from their own foundational values to guide them. Those are what constrain them and drive them—the core values to which they dedicate themselves and by which they are sustained.

DISCOVERING YOUR TRUE SELF

The question each of us really needs to answer is this, "What are the values that define my *true self*?" Discovery of our personal core values define who we really are, transform us, and bring peace, contentment, and a sense of purpose. So, how do we discover those core values that we will go to the mat for?

Here is what you do. Find a quiet time and place—mine is early in the morning when no one else is awake. Get your coffee or your tea and sit down to think. You will need a notebook to make notes. Think about the good times and the bad. Think about your victories and your defeats—your strengths and weaknesses. Think about your hopes and dreams.

As you begin the process, pay attention to the things that create passion in you—the ideas and personal qualities that are most important to you. Think of the times when you failed and felt bad about it. Personally, I key in on the feelings of regret for when I did something I was not proud of. For me, regret is a key to understanding there was a core value that I violated. It is a window to my soul and my true self.

When you discover those things that stir your soul, excite you, and generate a passion in you, pay attention. Write them down. This is the moment of discovery, the discovery of your true self.

There is one more thing. I want you to make an agreement with yourself, a contract, if you will. Ask yourself this question: What am I going to do about it? The thing you are going to do may be an action, or it may be a personal development need. For me, the motivation to write this book came out of just such an encounter that occurred at four-thirty one morning in my home in Houston. Whatever it is, *write down your plan and commit to executing it.* You may be able to handle doing so on your own, or you may need a coach or accountability partner—there is no right or wrong here.

One more thing I want you to know. This process is not an event—it's a journey that no one is too young or too old to embark upon.

Every person, woman or man, has inherent value, and every person has something to offer. Each of us has a unique story to write. There aren't many Martin Luthers nor are there many Martin Luther Kings. We are not all called to lead great movements or to change the world. However, we all have the opportunity each day to reach out, touch someone, and offer them a unique gift that can only come from the uniqueness of you. We all have the opportunity each day to make this world a better place. We all have the opportunity each day to stand up for the core values that define the best of who we are as a people.

PERSONAL RESPONSIBILITY TO ETHICALLY RESOLVE OUR PROBLEMS

The lessons I learned as a child have encrypted a code upon my heart. They erected in me an ethic that has served me well when the difficult seasons of life descended upon my family. It serves me well even today. Probably the greatest of these lessons is an understanding that there are things that are right and things that are just wrong. And when something is wrong, good men ought to do something about it.

Today our families and our nation are under great stress and in need of just such a code. In the face of a direct attack on the pillars of our republic, our leaders seem powerless to lead. Many just can't seem to get their careers out of the way of doing what is right. Now is the time for ordinary men and women to come forward for the sake of our nation. There are men and women of character in every walk of life and every town in this nation. They are found in every race, religion, and profession. The challenges we face today are calling us to greatness. It's time for us to do the right thing. This generation must answer for the kind of nation we leave to our children and our children's children. Like the boys on the beaches of Normandy, ordinary men and women are called to rise, to lead our nation, and restore our national pride.

We have serious problems and we need serious men to solve them. Our fellow citizens are not the enemy, regardless of how it may appear when vocal minorities living at both extremes start yelling at us and telling us how evil we all are. Those who label our fellow citizens with the most offensive terms they can dream up need to be replaced by dignified men and women who can carefully weigh the evidence and make reasoned decisions. Incivility will only serve to breed more incivility. When someone leaves the arena of ideas and debate, and launches a personal attack on another human being with the most despicable name they can come up with, then they will have doomed their cause and degraded themselves. We must have higher standards than that.

Giving more resources to government or any organization to solve the problems often drains the resources away from the very people who can affect real solutions. Worse yet, turning to an outside organization to solve our problems can serve to relieve us of our personal responsibility to act. The capacity of politics and bureaucracy to make substantive change in the way we deal with each other is limited. Human behavior can only be affected by getting at inner belief systems. We the people need to think for ourselves, come up with our own solutions, and fix things in our own communities.

How do we do that? I'm glad you asked. It begins with holding ourselves to a higher standard. It begins with men assuming their rightful role, defending that which is right, and upholding a system of values. It begins with each of us making a personal commitment to do what is best for our country, regardless of how it may impact our personal interest. Most important, it begins with seeing each other as people and not through the lens of some arbitrary label.

Finally, there are four important principles that I would like to highlight here:

- There is no possible outcome or personal agenda that is righteous enough to justify trampling on the rights of others.
- Never violate the principles of fairness, truth, civility, honor, or deliberately construct a solution you know has no chance of working.
- Vacating your responsibility to act with propriety or deal with others from a position of fairness and objectivity is never justified by the inappropriate behavior of others.
- A higher level of responsibility is required of those who have been endowed with greater portions of wealth, power, and influence.

Real progress happens when we objectively look at the facts as they are and dedicate ourselves to finding solutions that work.

True masculinity embraces these concepts, and models them with personal behavior. Your true self emanates from you like the light from a lighthouse, unwavering and reliable. Like the lighthouse that puts out a consistent beam, a person's true self can only be seen when it emanates from how one is truly made. The uniqueness of you combines with your code of standards to make up the true self that is you. It is only when one remains faithful to one's true self that a life of contentment, peace, and purpose is achieved. When that light begins to waver, it is time to stop and check ourselves to make sure we are being true to our code.

CHAPTER 3 REVIEW QUESTIONS

1. What are the core principles that define your true self? Hint: When we violate these core principles, we feel bad about ourselves.

2. What value is found in the concepts of fidelity, faithfulness, loyalty, commitment, and devotion?

3. What single core standard is the one that drives you and sustains you through life?

4. Being very honest with yourself, what are the areas of your life where your light wavers and you are not being true to who you are?

5. In looking at your life, what are the blessings you have received and what are you compelled to do in response?

6. Construct a personal development plan to begin living out the core of your true self. What are your standards? Where are they strong? What needs to be strengthened? How do they define your purpose?

CHAPTER 4

IN SEARCH OF DESTINY

*The two greatest days of your life are the day you
are born and the day you find out why.*
—Unknown
(Attributed to Mark Twain)

Mark Twain was a nineteenth-century American writer who is
considered by many to be America's greatest author. His books,
The Adventures of Huckleberry Finn and The Adventures of Tom
Sawyer, are considered American classics.

Mark Twain grew up in Hannibal, Missouri, on the banks of the
Mississippi River where he, like many of his friends, admired the men
who worked the steamboats on the river. He once wrote that "there
was but one permanent ambition"[7] among his friends—to be a steam-
boat man. He trained to be a river boat pilot under Horace Bixby, and
learned the river between St Louis and New Orleans. He worked as a
pilot on that section of river until the Civil War broke out and curtailed
traffic on the Mississippi. Although as a boy, being a riverboat pilot
seemed to be the greatest of all occupations, Twain found his greatest
calling as a writer. The day he realized that, was the second greatest
day of his life.

This idea of a second greatest day in our lives is pretty interesting, particularly when we think of a man who started out with the aspiration to be a riverboat pilot and wound up being a writer. There are lots of examples of people who experienced that second greatest day of their life that we could point to. Winston Churchill discovered that day when he stood on the floor of Parliament and rallied the people of Great Britain to stand against the Nazis with the words, "We shall Never Surrender." Abraham Lincoln, I believe, found that day when he signed his name at the bottom of the Emancipation Proclamation. Rosa Parks discovered her day when she sat down on the bus and refused to give up her seat.

These are all great historical figures. But what about people like you and me—the ordinary people?

JOURNEY OF DISCOVERY

Let me tell you a story about two friends of mine and how they found the second greatest day in their lives.

This couple owned a small business in partnership with the husband's family. They worked diligently to build their business, making the sacrifices that all small business owners make. After years of hard work, they found themselves in a position to live life however they chose. They could have chosen to travel and fill their lives with recreation. But instead, they chose to invest in a ranch and start an organization whose sole purpose was to help people save their marriages.

Over the years, hundreds of people have come to the ranch, spent five amazing days of counseling, and salvaged their hurting marriages. Some of these marriages were on the brink of dissolving. The success rate of the program is phenomenal. The joy my friends experience when lives are healed is a thing to behold, it is the thing that drives them. Their website is *www.intensives.com.* Read about what they do, and you will see a good example of two people who found the reason they were born. If your marriage is struggling, give them a call. They can help.

This second greatest day, the true reason for the "why" we were born, is something we call destiny. It is something we all have within us. We were born with it, we own it. Destiny is where we find our purpose and our highest calling. Contentment and fulfillment are to be found in its pursuit. Interestingly, when one encounters it, one always seems to discover the personal resources needed to fulfill that purpose.

Simply put, the road to destiny is the process of becoming the person you were meant to be, and accomplishing that for which you were made. This process of discovery is one of life's greatest adventures.

Success is based on two essential life positions:

- The willingness to attempt that which is difficult, things "they" said could not be done
- An absolute commitment to finish what is started regardless of the obstacles one encounters.

"I can't" and "I quit" are your enemies in this quest. If you desire to be a person of influence, then you must eradicate those two phrases from your thinking. In the following chapters, we will examine the transformation one experiences in life's storms, and the absolute value of failure. Those concepts and the concepts here will complete your Destiny Toolbox.

In the summer of 1776, Thomas Jefferson set forth what is arguably history's greatest statement of a nation's purpose. He set forth the principle that governments derive their just powers through the consent of the governed. That idea was new, in fact revolutionary. He declared that human rights are inalienable and derived from the Creator's endowment. With this document in hand, our Founding Fathers gathered in Philadelphia to usher in a new nation on the North American continent. A nation conceived in freedom and dedicated to the liberty of all men. Here's the rub—the 56 signers of the Declaration were not perfect. In fact, they were a long way from it, just like you and me. And they were really consumed with committing high treason as they declared our nation's independence. In the midst of proclaiming that all men are created equal, many of our people were left in terribly unequal positions. Many Americans were so unequal they were literally owned by other Americans. It would take a hundred years and another war to fix the inequality of slaves, and even longer for women.

I think this is a good place to talk about how we see and judge our ancestors. It is easy to look at men who lived in times past and judge them according to a code of conduct by which we should hold each other today. However, they lived in a different time and they lived in a different world, and they had to deal with issues that we don't have to deal with today. It helps to understand that we stand on the shoulders of people who came before us. We stand taller because we stand on what they built. It is far healthier to look at the good they did rather than what they got wrong, and appreciate our opportunity to benefit from the fruits of their labors. When my days are done, I hope I will be remembered for the good I've done rather than for the shortcomings of my life.

The concept of fatherhood reaches far beyond the family. Operating from integrity and wisdom, the Founding Fathers unleashed a power the likes of which the world had rarely seen—the power of human purpose, the concept that the average man should not be confined to a life dictated by the circumstances of his birth.

The power of the American spirit had been unshackled. In so doing, the greatest system of self-government and economic prosperity the world had ever seen was birthed. Our nation became the light of the world, and people from all over sought to come here to find a better way of life, to embrace the rewards of liberty and freedom. We became a nation that would go to war, defeat tyranny, voluntarily give the country back to its people, and finance the rebuilding. Consider the Marshall Plan, what we contributed to rebuild the Western European economies in the aftermath of World War 2, and you will discover the true greatness of the American people.

Pretty amazing don't you think? We are still a great nation because we are a great people.

In succeeding generations, after each major step forward to equality, people began to believe that a man could be or do anything he set his mind to. Such was the way it was in my family. The idea that I could do anything I set my mind to was not an empty concept. In our home was a man who had overcome all odds to live an accomplished life, to reach out and grab opportunity with both hands. The idea that I could accomplish anything I wanted was demonstrated every day by the man I most admired and aspired to emulate.

Consider this man, climbing to the top of a one-hundred-fifty foot tall distillation tower on a precarious ladder bolted to the side, and doing it with only one good leg. Think of the day when, as a child, his parents carried him out of the hospital with a completely paralyzed right leg hanging limply at his side. Now fast forward 20 years and picture that child as a young man standing at the bottom of the ladder, looking up, knowing that he had to climb to the top. Imagine the uncertainty that gripped him and the fear that it generated. How could somebody the doctors said would never walk be able to do that? Simple. It was because he decided he could do anything he set his mind to. Would you like to know something else? He was right. And guess what? You, too, can do anything you set your mind to if you just do not give up, but press through until you have attained the destiny for which you were born. This will be your ultimate victory.

What are the inner qualities that enable us to overcome fear and fuel our climb to the top? The tipping point is when we decide to engage.

It is the *strength of our character* that commissions us to face the challenge straight on, to leave safe harbor if you will. The persistence to continue until the ultimate victory is gained requires a different kind of capacity. It is the undeterred *determination of will* that drives us until we have conquered the thing that stands between us and our highest calling. These qualities reside in each of us and are waiting to be unlocked.

CHOOSING TO RISK A JOURNEY TO DISCOVER OUR HIGHEST PURPOSE

So, what is this thing we call destiny? To understand it, we must first understand that destiny is not found in the safest of places. It is found by those who are willing to take a risk and endure the struggle. Consider a ship. The safest place for a ship is in harbor, but that is not its place of highest purpose. A ship must put to sea and endure the risk of destruction to fulfill the builders' intended use.

In the same way, we are all endowed with a purpose higher than can be achieved by seeking safety and security. Our highest purpose is found when we decide to invest in the unknown. If we let the fear of failure prevent us from trying, we deprive ourselves of knowing whether or not we could have attained greatness. The power to achieve is drawn from the strength that resides deep in our soul. The privilege of fulfilling purpose is reserved for those with the courage to risk everything in pursuit of it.

Everyone who chooses to seek their destiny will be faced with two unavoidable obstacles. First, as the journey begins there is a great deal of uncertainty, and we really don't know where we are going. Determining where we wish to go is the genesis of growth. It is life's quintessential quest to learn who we are and to delineate our guiding principles.

Second to that growth is the struggle. Consider a baby bird as it fights to break free from its shell. The drive for life causes it to break out of a safe and nurturing place and face the fear of the unknown.

Interestingly, if the baby bird were to stay in that safe place inside the shell, it would starve to death. As the bird breaks the shell away, it struggles with all the strength it can muster to free itself.

For the baby bird, to break into the unknown is a genetically controlled instinct, performed without thought. For us, giving up residence in our own comfort zone is an act we must make consciously. If we want to achieve our highest purpose, we must deliberately choose the risk. Such is the struggle we must endure to find our true place.

There will be times when you do not think you have the strength to carry on, and may doubt that you have chosen the right path. Guaranteed, at some point you will be faced with a storm that you must choose either to weather or to avoid. Invariably, turning back or skirting around possible hardship will lead you away from your destiny.

It is in these times that we are faced with a deeply personal choice. A simple one, really, but one that often passes virtually unnoticed: Are we going to continue the struggle, or are we going to give up?

We must learn to consciously look for and recognize these opportunities for growth.

Examine my father as a child learning to walk with one good leg, and we will see an example of a choice well made. He was faced with that choice thousands of times in his life. He always made the choice to continue, to keep going until he had nothing left to give. It was only then that success was his, that he became the victor. And because he had normalized making that difficult choice, it became automatic.

Something in him whispered that allowing himself to quit would destroy him. He knew it in his gut. And there was something else, even more threatening. He knew that once he chose to quit, it would become easier the next time he was faced with life's obstacles.

The choice to quit has the potential to destroy us, as well, in our quest for destiny. A person cannot reach his highest purpose if he chooses the easy way out, or if he decides to give up on himself.

Fatherhood has a purpose in this moment of personal choice, in the choices our children make, and the choices we make as a nation. It is our place always to encourage the right choice, to council and provide the wisdom we have gleaned from our own journey. Most important, it is our job as fathers to demonstrate a way of life that our children can draw upon to find the strength they need when they are faltering. The way we live our lives speaks louder than the words we utter. The life a father lives and the principles he teaches are the lighthouse beams that show our children the best course as they navigate life's troubled waters.

I want to share something with you, and it's something that is deeply personal. It has to do with the battle for my mind. My greatest struggle in the pursuit of my destiny has come from within myself. It was a nagging thought that I just didn't have what it takes. That negative thought persisted in the face of the very lessons my father, by his word and his life, sought to teach me. He gave voice to it when he would tell me, "Gary, can't never could do anything." He put action to it in the way he faced his physical limitations.

I think many of us have those self-doubts. I suspect I'm not alone and that many of us feel that way. Our greatest victories will be gained when we overcome the highest obstacles our minds erect.

THE PLACE OF HIGHEST PURPOSE

There is one more thing about the quest for life's highest purpose, and it is central to the struggle. The ultimate purpose for our lives waits for us on the other side of our greatest challenge. Destiny resides on the other side of that one thing we fear the most, past the place of our most intense feeling of inadequacy.

There is a reason for this. The very lessons we need to learn to achieve our life's purpose are found in struggle and weakness. The courage gleaned from facing down our fears enable us to take on the unknown. Just as important, the journey through life's obstacles and fears will bring us to a place where a deep sense of self-satisfaction can be enjoyed.

Hurt and pain are part and parcel of the experiences that transform and uniquely equip each of us to fulfill the purpose for which we were designed. The hurts and pains gathered along life's journey persist as they are stored in our hearts. Inner healing does what it can, but memories often remain that flare up in refreshed pain at the most inopportune moments. Ultimate healing is found when we understand the purpose of the pain in the journey to our destiny.

By focusing on the purpose of pain in equipping us for our calling and advancing us in our chosen arena, we bring the distress into proper perspective. It is then that we find the ultimate healing in our hearts and learn to revel in the journey of life. The purpose of the struggle comes into clear focus when we finally stand on the mountain of achievement at the center of our destiny. We may find great joy here, and truly say that it was worth all the pain.

It is in the heart of the struggle where we discover what we are made of, and it is in facing down our fears that we gain the courage to walk into the unknown. If we commit ourselves to persisting no matter what the odds, and we put pain in proper perspective, then we gain the chance to write our story the way it was meant to be written.

Destiny is found in the moment of deeply personal choice, the choice to venture into the unknown and face down whatever obstacle may come your way. It is your choice to make, and your choice alone. It is your destiny, and you get to decide what you will do with it. But never ever think that you're not important, and you don't have a valuable place in this world. I assure you, you have everything it takes to be all that you were meant to be, and you were designed for wonderful things.

CHAPTER 4 REVIEW QUESTIONS

1. Consider adopting a habit of embracing the difficult things in your life and finishing what you start. How would this impact your quest for destiny?

2. Do "I can't" or "I quit" play any part in your thinking? If so, can you see where rejecting the concepts would make things better for you? Explain.

3. Are there places of comfort you are holding onto that are hindering your quest for purpose? Give specific examples.

4. Examine where you are weak and where you struggle. What are some opportunities for personal developmental you can see there?

5. Where are you in your personal pursuit of your "second greatest day?" What principles in this chapter do you think might help you?

6. Assess the role that pain has played in your pursuit of purpose. What was it amid the pain and struggle that changed you and prepared you for the pursuit of purpose?

7. Develop a destiny strategy. It should be written and contain an assessment of the following:

   a. Clear statement of your purpose. Think of this as your mission statement.

   b. An honest assessment of your strengths and weaknesses.

   c. A complete list of the things from your past that are making you think you can't achieve your destiny.

   d. A list of personal development needs, and resources you need to achieve your purpose.

CHAPTER 5

THE MEASURE OF A MAN

Down these mean streets a man must go who is himself not mean, who is neither tarnished nor afraid. He is the hero; he is everything. He must be a complete man and a common man and yet an unusual man. He must be, to use a rather weathered phrase, a man of honor—by instinct, by inevitability, without thought of it, and certainly without saying it. He must be the best man in the world and good enough for any world.[8]
—*Raymond Chandler*

What are we to make of these beings we call men, and what, in real terms, are the qualities they require to attain the full stature of their essential natures?

When a man takes on the full measure of his manhood, he is empowered to be a true father and positively change the world around him. In this chapter, we will examine the qualities of healthy manhood, a man's vital role in advancing and sustaining our civilization, the propriety with which he is to conduct himself, and the restraint on his power which he is bound by honor to self-impose.

A man is a person who is secure in what he believes, bases those beliefs on sound fundamentals, and controls his emotions to make decisions based on reason and sound judgment. He is able to get outside his personal needs and act in a manner that sustains and advances the world around him.

Overlay these qualities with the heart of a father, and you introduce the man's concern for the well-being of *all* those in his sphere of influence.

The partnership of manhood and fatherhood is a potent combination.

THE DIMENSIONS OF AUTHENTIC MANHOOD

In these troubled times, true men are needed to step to the forefront and lead us out of the endless cycle of useless accusation and recrimination. The need is for strong men who can look past the roar, assess the problems as they really are, and come up with reasoned solutions. Solutions that actually work.

Our nation needs authentic men to model examples of what true manhood is. These men must be dedicated to doing the right thing, no matter the cost. They must possess an uncommon portion of the qualities I describe as strength of character and determination of will. Authentic men must be dedicated to the proposition of perfecting the manhood within themselves and deploying that trustworthy masculinity into their unique spheres of influence.

In today's world, how are we to recognize men such as these?

I believe they can be identified by the qualities demonstrated by their lives. Let me give you a few of the key qualities I think are essential.

- **Inner Strength** is the quality that allows a man to set his course based on his core values, unmoved by events or the opinions of others. This is like the captain of a sailing ship who has the skill and temperament to sail his ship into the wind. True masculinity looks inward for the resolution of problems. Men who possess it are self-reliant, and reject the concept that they need someone else for support and affirmation.

- **Self-Awareness** is when inner strength combines with maturity and self-confidence to free a man to be honest about who he is. A self-aware man has a clear understanding of his strengths and weaknesses. He rejects the notion that he needs to cover weakness with a false façade. He uses this awareness to competently manage his life.

- **Authenticity** is the outer genuineness that validates the true nature of the inner man. Truly authentic people mean what they say, and they say what they mean. When paired with good character, this quality can lead to a highly effective life because it breeds trust within those who deal with them.

- **Objectivity** is the attribute that empowers a person to look through an issue and see what is right, true, and just, regardless of whether that supports his own personal positions. A good example of this is a judge who can look at the facts and objectively rule on what the law says, regardless of whether or not he personally agrees. This quality is essential in a man who is dealing with difficult issues between conflicting interests, each of which have some validity. Objectivity is the quality that compels him to support the view that is merited, even when it is diametrically opposed to that which he holds most dear. In these days when we as a people are so polarized, the need for objective men on both sides is critical.

- **Resolve** is the act of will when a person decides what he believes, based on a definition of right and wrong and his inner value system. Resolve is not moved by pressure to conform to any ideology, nor is it deterred by external resistance. Resolve represents the internal force that drives us to take on every challenge that presents itself, and causes us to persist until we have overcome whatever life throws at us.

- **Propriety** defines how a man conducts himself. It encompasses the concepts of decorum, respectability, correctness, decency, courtesy, morality, civility, and modesty. A man who possesses it rises above his own internal struggles and his personal weaknesses to act in a respectful manner. A man infused with this quality raises the level of discourse of all those around him, creates a zone of safety where everyone's unique contributions are realized, and maximizes advancement. Propriety is essential to the dynamics of teams, as it restrains behaviors which would tear a team apart.

- **Courage** is the strength to do what is right in the face of almost certain retribution. A good example of this is Atticus Finch in the novel *To Kill a Mockingbird*. In the story, he defended a black man who had been unjustly accused of a crime, even knowing he would reap the ire of the local townspeople. Atticus was unmoved—he staked out his position and would not be deterred. Courage empowers us to fight the good fight without reservation, to wade into the maelstrom, and confront our worst fears.

- **Understanding** is the quality that allows one to encounter one's fellow men, look deeply into them, see them for who they really are, and deal with them in a way that brings out the best in everyone. It encompasses a life position that fully embraces the essential value of every human being, and understands that we are all diminished when we lose any one person's unique contribution. Understanding enables us to keep our eyes on the end goal and ignore the noise of the unimportant.

- **Wisdom** is a rare quality that comes with experience and a consistent dedication to making good decisions. In reality, it is often derived of learning from one's mistakes. Wisdom knows when it is time to act and when it is time to be restrained. A wise man consistently overcomes his emotions and makes reasoned decisions. He also has the uncanny ability to see forward and quickly assess the future impact of actions made today.

True manhood empowers us to live according to these qualities and to deal with our fellow man from a position of compassion, because we are secure in our manhood and not bound to an unhealthy code that requires us to prove that we are men. True manhood rejects overaggressive behaviors that seek to dominate all that is around them.

Clearly, the call here is for men to aspire to the highest standard of masculinity. This is not a call to return to an earlier time, as that would require us to accept the deficiencies of the past. But rather to embrace and perfect the best qualities of manhood. This is a call for men who are willing to walk the mean streets and be, as Raymond Chandler said, "neither tarnished nor afraid."[8] Men who are not bullies, but rather who step out of the crowd to confront the bully.

Some would urge men to become more feminine in order to right the abuses they perceive as products of masculinity itself. It does no one any good for men to abandon the concept of manhood in a vain effort to reverse abuse, for the pain of abused cries out to the strength of authentic men for justice and protection. It is, however, vital that we as men confront abuse with the essential strength of our masculinity. Government is largely powerless to set right the wrongs of abuse. So, here's the deal. There are things going on that are just wrong, and somebody ought to do something about it.

Men, that somebody is you.

FUNDAMENTALS OF MANHOOD

Manhood is a quality that is very difficult to define, but we seem to know it when we see it. I know what it looks like because I sat at the dinner table every day of my youth with a person who embodied it.

Still, it can be hard to describe. Sometimes we are left with describing what it's *not*. Reminds me of a day in graduate school when our professor challenged us to come up with a description of a cat that fully described a cat and nothing else. After about forty-five minutes, the students gave up, unsuccessful. We were good at describing a cat, it's just that our descriptions described other things, as well.

Here are my characteristics that describe a cat—covered in fur, a tail at the back, head in front, four legs, two ears on top of its head, two eyes, one nose, one mouth, it feeds its young with milk, five claws on the front feet and four on the back, when it drinks water it laps it up with its tongue. That should do it—right? Do you know what else this describes—a dog.

Now, that should tell us something. For starters, being a taxonomist is really hard. It should also illustrate how problematic it is to come up with labels that define people. I will see if I can do better as I attempt to describe what a real man is, and what makes him unique and indispensably valuable.

There are genetics involved here, which govern much more than physical attributes. In general, men have distinct physical traits, some of which can be confusing—like why our hair falls out when we can still grow a beard. We can't have babies, nor do we possess the ability to produce the food they need. We can, however, draw on our natural physical strengths to endure long hours of physical labor to provide.

There are also certain things attached to the Y chromosome that make men unique in more ways than just physicality. Any attempt to ignore these things will cause frustration and meet with determined resistance, and so it should. There are attributes of mental toughness, aggression, and assertiveness, as well as an inner demand for respect that will drive us to fight for it. Healthy men embrace their masculinity, are motivated to provide, and gain self-respect and fulfillment when we succeed. We are driven to protect, with the innate instinct to turn toward danger and confront it. This is all instinctual.

The mental picture I would paint for you is this. Visualize a family out in public being attacked by an assailant. Chances are, the mother's instinct will be to look for the children, gather them to her, and place herself between them and the attacker. The father's instinct is to turn toward the assailant, rush toward him, and take him down. He is driven by aggressive protectiveness and righteous anger to defend those he loves. Together, each parent protects their family in a perfect, complimentary way.

I remember nights when my dad with his one good leg stood up to his sister's husband who was threatening her. Her husband was a former marine who had an alcohol problem and got violent when he was drunk. My dad knew he couldn't win in a fight, but something welled up in him, he stood his ground, and protected his sister. That something was the quality in him that was his true manhood. He was a man as Raymond Chandler described when he said: "*Down these mean streets a man must go who is himself not mean, who is neither tarnished nor afraid. He is the hero.*"[8] My dad was my hero and he was neither afraid nor tarnished. He was a man…and I was safe. I had my model and I had his genetics. I am uncommonly lucky and proud to be called his son.

CRITICAL NEED FOR FATHERS

Marriages these days are failing at an alarming rate. Invariably, it is a painful experience for everyone, particularly the children. Rebuilding a struggling marriage is a daunting task and will only work if both parties work closely together, expressing mutual respect, and are dedicated to assuring that the children love and respect both parents. This same spirit of cooperation, respect, and focus on the children's needs is essential if the marriage dissolves and one parent leaves the home. If one or both parents extract vengeance by tearing down each other, the children will be wounded and their identities damaged.

I understand that there are single mothers and single dads doing a great job, and there are fathers living outside the home that stay involved with their children. If you are a man who finds himself separated from his children, I challenge you to stay involved with them, and vigilantly be for them what you only can be. If men do not stay engaged in their lives, children are destined to live in an environment where they get an imbalanced view of masculinity and femininity. In the category of undeniable truth, children learn much more by what they see than what they hear. The absence of a stable male presence is unhealthy for children as they grow up, trying to understand the proper roles of males and females.

It is imperative we understand there are far too many children being raised without a good father. As a result, there are far too many with a father-shaped hole in their souls, thus producing far too many broken boys and girls.

I suspect if we dig down deep into our society's most troubling problems, we can find the dysfunctionality of fatherhood as a root cause. There is a critical role in building the fabric of a good and just society that can be filled only by a father. I would challenge all men everywhere to step forward and fill the role of fatherhood for which they are responsible. I would challenge men everywhere to seek out the fatherless, help heal their hurts, and fill the hole in their soul with your presence. Often the simple thought that someone cares is transformative.

At this point you may be wondering why society should be so passionate about empowering men to be men and equipping them to be fathers. Let me share with you something I learned from a friend of mine. He travels extensively in third world countries and meets with governmental leaders. He goes to places like Central Africa where years of war and genocide have taken their toll and wiped out entire generations. He tells me there are leaders who have told him they literally have no fathers in their countries. Adult men are either dead or permanently away fighting. As a result, their young men don't know what a true father looks like. It's hard to emulate what one doesn't see.

In our country, more and more children are being raised in homes without fathers. I am passionate about this subject because I fear this trend will continue, and we may be in danger of suffering the same fate as those other countries.

DYSFUNCTIONAL CONCEPTS OF MANHOOD

Within the category of what a man is *not* resides a lot of wrong thinking about manhood.

To some, a man is someone who can take whatever he wants through his misplaced physical, financial, or positional advantage. It is this misguided exercise of power that describes a person who is the antithesis of a man.

To others, a man is a person adept at convincing a girl or woman to surrender her trust and intimacy for his momentary pleasure. A real man does not take advantage of people who find themselves in a tough spot. That describes machoism, not manhood.

Doubtless, some think it's manly to manipulate and force women to cater to their wants, but true manhood means never putting oneself into a place of superiority, or roughly exercising one's authority for self-ish purposes...or for any purpose. Manhood is not about using fear and intimidation to control those around you. Behaviors such as these run counter to the concept of manliness.

Rather than strength, those characteristics are a sign of weakness and insecurity, and more appropriately describe a bully or a weakling. In this day of social media and the internet, bullying has taken on an entirely new dimension, enabled by the ability to remain anonymous. Bullying has become rampant. The statistics for middle school students tells us that one in three-to-four children find themselves the target of bullying (www.stopbullying.gov). A bully is much different than a man, because there is no honor in that kind of behavior.

Today, the need for true masculinity has never been more acute.

INNER STRENGTH AND MENTAL TOUGHNESS

In Randy Travis' song "Three Wooden Crosses,"[9] there's a line that says, "It's not what you take when you leave the world behind you. It's what you leave behind you when you're gone."

A real man is measured by his care for the weak and by the legacy he leaves behind. A real man will inevitably turn to his code of dignity for guidance in life. His is an inner strength derived from knowing who he is and where he stands. His feet are planted deep in the soil of that which is right and forged by a life well-lived. A real man clearly understands what is right and what is wrong, but more important, he has the practiced will to temper his own behavior to conform to those principles. He will dedicate himself to the premise of defending the right and defeating the wrong.

The propriety of a man's actions is a window into his inner self. The full expression of his character can be found in the compassion and understanding with which he exercises his power and authority.

Mental toughness is an essential quality of a real man. By toughness I mean an inner quality which drives a man to stand his ground in tough times. Toughness empowers a man to drive a stake in the ground and declare, "This is where I stand." It is the quality that empowers a man to find a way through the hard times, to press on and not forsake his principles. Toughness compels a man to take on what is before him simply because it is the right thing to do. Men with this controlling motivation don't need anyone to tell them what to do, but take the initiative on their own.

This idea of mental toughness encompasses the concepts of courage and loyalty. A prime example is that of the men who rode the Higgins Boats onto Omaha Beach on June 6, 1944. They charged straight into a hail of German gunfire with incredible courage and a loyalty to each other that was unfathomable. They went in to rescue the weak from oppressive tyranny. To them, ultimate failure meant abandoning the brother next to them. Failing to uphold a responsibility to their brother in arms was so abhorrent they risked everything to guard against it. They cherished honor, and defended it with their very lives.

THE COMPETENCE OF MANHOOD

The last concept I want to discuss is that of competence. There is more to be said later, but I want to link some things together here.

If you aspire to be a grown man, to live a life of influence, and appeal to that special young lady, you need a full complement of personal, occupational, and financial competence. A woman with a healthy self-image is not attracted to a man who cannot earn a good living and cannot take care of his money. Financial incompetence is not the mark of a man, and is deeply unattractive.

Intertwined with all this is the importance of knowing who you are and being secure in yourself. Competence and security in who you are is critical, and one of the first things most women look for in a man. That is, the quality of personal competence. In many ways, a man is defined by his proficiency in his chosen occupation. This is an important component of his self-image. When we are comfortable in our occupation, it comes across as confidence to those you deal with. For the sake of your mental well-being, it is critical to nurture competence in all aspects of your life.

PRACTICAL GUIDANCE

If I may be so bold, I 'd like to offer some practical suggestions for the young ladies out there.

Recently, I was sitting on the outdoor patio of my favorite slightly-upscale restaurant, within easy view of the front door. A guy walked in wearing a sleeveless T-shirt, a pair of baggy sports shorts, flip flops, and a ball cap worn backward. I guess to him, the ball cap was what completed this amazing ensemble. Following behind him was an attractive young lady who had clearly put out an effort to look nice. Her hair looked freshly styled, and she wore dark denim and high heels. The pair didn't look like they were together, but to my shock, he opened the door and made a cursory effort to hold it behind him until she could reach out to hold it for herself. He was wearing a look I can only describe as total self-absorption.

I later saw them at the bar looking at their phones, no conversation. I wouldn't be surprised if she had to pay for her food. I understand from some of my younger friends that these days, a guy who will buy dinner is a real game-changer. There are a lot of good reasons a young lady would want to pay for her own meal. But if you are going to lay claim to being a man, the least you can do is offer to foot the bill when a woman has already spent so much time and money to look nice for you. As for a man who never offers to pay... Are you kidding me?

Young ladies, why do you put up with that foolishness? You aren't dealing with real men, that's for sure. Next time you go out, make him pay, make him open the car door, and make him hold the door to the restaurant open for you. Set the expectation, and if he doesn't rise to the occasion, don't waste your time on him.

Here's how you can do this. When you walk out to the car, just stand there until he opens the door for you. If he gets in and sits down and you are standing there expectantly, he'll get the message. If he walks into a building in front of you like the guy I saw, don't reach out to catch the door. Just let it close and stand there. He will be so curious as to what you're doing that he'll come back. Then politely inform him that if he wants to hang with you, he is going to have to up his game and to start treating you with more respect. At this point give him about forty-five seconds to overcome his shock and respond appropriately. Otherwise, tell him you have an Uber app on your phone.

If he steps up, this would be a good time to inform him he should also dress better when he goes out with you. If he doesn't have a conversion experience, request the Uber. Don't worry about getting another date. The guy you really want will know how to respect you. They are definitely out there, so don't settle for less than you deserve.

For the young man interested in finding this young lady, I have some pointers about how a real man treats a woman. Give them a try. The girl you're looking for is likely just waiting for a real man to show up.

- Develop your professional and financial competence
- The girl you want is not looking for the town's Greatest Video Game Player
- Make a woman feel safe, protect her bodily autonomy, treat her with respect
- Open the door for her at the car and restaurant like a normal respectful gentleman
- If you really want to be a radical, open the door for a complete stranger
- If you're taking her to dinner, go where she likes
- If you don't know where that is, ask her best friend
- Here is a tip—do that and her best friend will immediately call her friend and tell her—that would be a good thing
- Be a man and offer to pay for her dinner
- Leave your cell phone in your pocket; she deserves your undivided attention
- Look her in the eyes and have an actual conversation
- Do not let her out dress you
- Have the courage to ask her for an actual date. The lame "let's hang out" suggestion is for cowards—be upfront about your intentions
- When you go to pick her up, walk up to her door and knock. Only getaway drivers honk
- Clean your car, which tells her she's important

Yes, these tips may sound archaic, but there is a good reason. The art of being a gentleman is fast becoming a lost art. I challenge you to do as I've suggested. If you want to find that special young lady, this is a good start. The right one will love you for it. You young guys should be thankful I'm old and married. If I were young and single, I'd clean your clock!

CHAPTER 5 REVIEW QUESTIONS

1. Discuss the partnership between manhood and fatherhood and how each facet contributes to the potency of the partnership.

2. Examine the key qualities of manhood in the bulleted list early in this chapter and rate yourself against those.

3. Evaluate your strengths and weaknesses and what can you do personally to enhance these qualities within you.

4. How do the qualities of aggressiveness and toughness tempered by reason and restraint blend to define a real man?

5. Think about your drive for respect and how your desire to protect and provide contribute to your self-respect. Explain.

6. What qualities of manhood empower a man to protect the weak?

7. Thinking about the problem of cyber-bullying, what are the causes, effects, solutions, and the role that empowering true manhood could play?

8. Look forward to the end of your time on earth. What do you want to leave behind as your legacy?

CHAPTER 6

PROTECTION, PROVISION, PERSEVERANCE

The ultimate test of a moral society is the kind of world that it leaves to its children.
—*Attributed to Dietrich Bonhoeffer*

Fundamental values form the underpinnings of our culture and stem from a core drive to advance and succeed. These values are at the center of mankind's burning need to be better tomorrow than we are today. They bind us together as we walk the journey of life, and make us better together than we are alone. If properly derived and faithfully executed, core values become the facilitating belief system upon which culture progresses. The health and well-being of culture depends upon a self-driven adherence to shared values by the people who live in the culture.

This chapter examines the three core values of protection, provision, and perseverance that are key to the fundamental health of fatherhood.

Let us be clear on the point that no one lives in isolation, no one walks the journey of life alone. The health of the society into which we are born is critical. We can do a good job of raising our own children and developing a functional personal belief system within them, only to see them damaged by the world around them.

This is why we need to attain a critical mass of healthy fatherhood. Maintenance of cultural health depends on empowering people of influence who are dedicated to the selfless nurturing of the civilization. The absence of a mutually dedicated group of individuals, who are committed to a value-based society, will negate the efforts of a few individuals who are. As responsible members of a healthy culture, we must restrain the dishonorable self-aggrandizement that arises from our base nature. We must put aside the devotion to self and turn our creative talents to the pursuit of the common good—for that is where the essential goodness of the human soul flourishes.

Since fathers form the foundation of the culture we are attempting to empower, we must understand clearly the meaning of these three core values. Although functional fatherhood is not the only requirement in society, it is an essential element, without which we will fail in our efforts.

Let us now examine each of these in the context of true manhood.

PROTECTION

If you recall, we talked about the instinctual response a man should have when those in his care are attacked. In many ways, the attack response spurs him to confront the danger with little regard for personal safety. This is not a thoughtful decision but rather a stimulus-response reaction that comes from the essence of his manhood.

This was the way it was in my family, and as a result, a place of safety and security was established. I never felt insecure or concerned given my father's handicap, because I never thought of him as handicapped. I never thought of him as weak because his physical limitations never kept him from protecting us. Yes, he had only one good leg, but he didn't allow that to stop him from standing up for us. And I absorbed it all as beautiful normalcy.

We had an issue in the family when I was a child—my aunt's husband had a drinking problem. I think he drank to numb the pain within himself. The first problem was that he often became violent when he'd had too much to drink. The second problem was that he was very strong. And it always seemed to be at night that an episode would arise. My dad's sister would call our house for help, and my dad would go. Here's the third problem—it is relatively easy to beat up a man with one leg. Or at least, one would think it's a problem. And yet, though I was never around to see it, my dad would go, the situation would be resolved, and he would come home. And that was all there was to it.

How was he able to face down someone of such superior strength? The answer was respect. In all aspects of my dad's life, he carried himself in a way that garnered respect from all those who knew him. As a result, his words carried an authority that impelled things to happen. He had this pleasant nature and an endearing smile that drew you to him. Yet, when the smile left his face, his eyes narrowed, determination showed up, and the game changed. When he said, "No," it came backed by an inner strength that arose from his character. I guess he learned early on the power contained in that two-letter word. Wonder where he got that from?

This was the atmosphere in which I grew up. Home was a place of safety where, in my father's arms, I felt the love that guaranteed my security. I knew that with him, there was always a place where nothing and no one could hurt me. When as a child, those most terrible of hurts were visited upon me, they would seem unbearable. However, when I walked in the back door of our home the hurt would melt away and be replaced by a father's love.

After he was gone, I had to face the world alone. I still had to deal with the same hurts that are thrust upon us all, but somehow, I always had a reservoir of inner strength that he had placed within me. That strength caused me to see each challenge for what it was. At age fifty-three he was gone, but he had done his job well.

We have been without him for forty years, but not a day goes by that I do not wish I could see that smiling face again. I live each day in the hope that I am worthy of having had him as my father. Each word I write is with the intent to honor that good man. The more time I spend writing this book, the more I understand how truly fortunate I was to have my twenty-seven years with him.

You may be asking, what qualities could garner that much respect? What caused people to seek his guidance when there was trouble in their lives or conflict with other people? What are the qualities he embodied which earned him the respect that he carried? What are the qualities that earned him the right to be a protector? They are:

- Impeccable integrity
- A dedication to trustworthiness
- Genuine interest in others' well-being
- Unquestioning truthfulness
- Indisputable honor

These are the qualities that reside in the innate goodness of all men, embryonic qualities just waiting to be called upon. These are the things which form the moral basis for personal authority and create a place of safety for the family.

I'd like to take a minute to acknowledge that while some of us had a good father experience, others did not. But if the latter is true, I want you to know that you also have full access to these virtues, even if you may have to work a little harder to identify them. The qualities described here are your birthright. They reside in each man and are there to be called out at will. They are your right, the right to be a true father—the right to be a true man. These, as all your rights, are unalienable, for they were endowed by your Creator.

PROVISION

Today we live in an age of dual-income families. Women have joined the work force *en masse* and hold responsible positions, just as men do. The unique qualities women bring to the table have enriched all our lives. The talents and creativity women possess are incredible. I shudder to think of the discoveries we have surely missed because women were on the sidelines for far too long.

However, it is still a foremost responsibility of the father to provide for the basic needs of his family. When times get tough, it is ultimately the father's responsibility to provide the firewall of food, clothing, transportation, and housing for his family. There are, to be sure, special circumstances that prevent a man from providing, and this is by no means a criticism of men who find themselves in such a position. Ultimately, each family must deal with life according to the situation they find themselves in.

Regardless, provision is one of those key roles in life that should not be neglected or delegated. I saw my father leave the house at six-thirty every morning, whether he felt like it or not. In fact, this was a role he sought as he charged off into life, determined to overcome his physical limitations. He took pride in the fact that he succeeded, and provided well for his family. His job frequently required him to climb to the top of one-hundred-fifty-foot distillation towers in a chemical plant, (see Chapter 4). The climb was straight up on a simple ladder bolted to the side of the column. It wasn't like most ladders that lean against a building at an angle, but went straight up. It was an exhausting climb for most able-bodied men as the position of your body is trying to push you back, away from the ladder, creating great stress on your shoulders and legs. But, Billy Ray did it and he did it with one good leg.

While writing this book, I discovered another thing about my father. Each time he stood at the bottom of that ladder, he didn't know if he could climb to the top. There was always a fear that he would get half way up and not go any further. The fear of uncertainty was heavy on him.

How do I know this? Because I had the same thoughts when I found myself in that same position. Years later, as I went to work in that same chemical plant and climbed those same towers, I found out what it was like. As I reached the top, exhausted and frightened by the height and dreading the descent, I finally realized what he had done for me every day of my life. At that moment, I learned the final lesson that would propel me into manhood and prepare me to provide for those entrusted to me.

For the record, climbing a ladder was something the doctors said he would never do. He consciously chose the job that required him to make such a climb and do it routinely. In his world, conquering the things they said were impossible was what charged him up. Being the family provider was his identity, his choice, and his joy.

PERSEVERANCE

Life is not a simple straight-line journey. In my experience, it's more like a maze where we plot our course, encounter obstacles, plot a course around them, and repeat—all the while trying to get to where we were going.

Here's one of the funny things about life. In the midst of all this, we sometimes forget where we were going in the first place. It is the quality of perseverance that steers us through such times and keeps us rooted. Perseverance is the quality that sustains a man until his roots grow deep, and which nurtures his children and gives them the stability they need to grow.

We observed an amazing example of perseverance as we walked through our Houston neighborhood in the aftermath of Hurricane Harvey in September 2017. Rows upon rows of mature, strong pine trees still stood tall and strong. The ground was littered with their needles and branches, but their deep, tenacious roots enabled them to withstand the torrential rain and wind. A robust tap root sunk deep into the soil maintains a tree against the strongest storms.

Likewise, a father's perseverance is there to help his children stay on course and avoid the detrimental effects of unintended consequence. More important, it is a father's duty to demonstrate through his life the quality of standing firm and strong in the face of opposition and in the midst of hardship. Unfortunately, too many children are the walking wounded because the father, the one who should provide an atmosphere of security, is absent or negligent.

A true father's role is to persevere on behalf of his children and demonstrate the strength that is needed to stand his ground with a resolve that cannot be thwarted. If we as fathers are constantly changing or disappearing, an atmosphere of insecurity develops within the family and our children do not know what to expect. Their fragile spirits can be easily broken without our strength to guide them.

So, men, what are we to do? Should we as men be willing to abandon our responsibilities and leave our children in a place where they are compelled to search elsewhere for the father's strength that they so desperately need? I think not. I believe abandoning this responsibility is unconscionable. Perseverance of standards and ethics are critical in helping our children toward their purpose.

However, there is another very important aspect to our families that helps our children take root, and that is tradition. Family traditions are vital in establishing a child's identity.

TRADITIONS

In our home, we established very clear traditions around Christmas. Our children came to understand that the way we did Christmas was always going to be the same. They knew that we were going to open presents on Christmas morning. They knew their mom was going to put great effort into their stockings, and that we would unload them before the presents. Our children were persistent in asking me every year if we could open one present on Christmas Eve. I always said, "No," and somehow, I think they would have been disappointed if I had said, "Yes."

Traditions are critical to the human experience. They are important to our understanding of who we are and what makes us belong. Traditions sustain the identity of a family and the identity of a nation. As a nation, when we gather for our great sporting events, we always begin with our national anthem. It serves to remind us of the reality that even though we are supporting different teams, we are gathered first and foremost as Americans. Somehow, I believe our Founding Fathers would be pleased with that.

Traditions bind us together and remind us there is more that unites us than divides us. How else to explain the way we come together in times of tragedy and times when our nation is attacked? How else to explain the dedication and valor of the men and women who go into battle to defend us?

I believe it is because we know who we are because of the common ground we share, and that we will persevere unto victory to keep that ground safe.

In a similar way, traditions that bind a family are multifaceted. They encompass all our ways—the way we celebrate special days, the way we maintain our belief systems, the way we live our lives. It falls to the perseverance of the family unit to sustain our traditions. It also falls to fathers to correct or suspend those traditions that are unhealthy or that harm the less fortunate.

The question is, how do we know the difference?

Our core values are vital in determining this difference, as well as establishing and preserving a healthy culture. Sustaining our culture is important, and is fueled by unselfish devotion to the common good, encompassed in the principles of protection, provision and perseverance.

These values form a place of security where the young grow into adulthood. When properly nurtured, children will stand strong in the knowledge of who they are and what their purpose is in life.

CHAPTER 6 REVIEW QUESTIONS

1. What benefits does society derive from adhering to a set of core values? How do we arrive at agreement on these values?
2. What are the inner qualities of a man that empower him to be a person to whom people can turn for counsel?
3. What role does the drive to provide play in manhood?
4. What qualities create an environment of security and safety? What qualities might compromise those?
5. What role do differing traditions play in the family and in the nation?

CHAPTER 7

TRANSFORMATION
IN THE STORM

Commandancy of the Alamo-
Bejar, Fby. 24ᵗʰ 1836
To the people Texas &
All Americans in the world

*…I have sustained a continual Bombardment & cannonade for 24 hours and I have not
lost a man — The enemy has demanded a surrender at discretion, otherwise the garrison
are to be put to the sword, if the fort is taken — I have answered the demand with
cannon shot & our flag still waves proudly from these walls I shall never surrender…*[10]
—*William Barrett Travis*
Lt. Col. comdt

The existential struggle of the human experience is an often unrelenting journey through life's critical experiences. Sometimes in
the hard times of life we come face-to-face with our purpose. Other
times, the role these critical moments have played only becomes clear
when reviewed in retrospect, and we come to understand that we were
changed in the midst of them.

William Barrett Travis certainly found himself in such a place in a crumbling mission near San Antonio de Bexar. Facing a great opposing army, he had few men and little provision. However, like the mythical phoenix, Texas later rose from the ashes of the Alamo. Remembering the sacrifice of these brave men became the clarion call for Texans as they stepped forward to claim their land and their liberty. Texans consider the Alamo sacred ground, consecrated by the bravery and blood of Travis and his men.

FINDING PURPOSE IN THE STRUGGLE

The journey to find purpose often passes through the high-stress seasons of life where our ability to endure is sorely tested and life's important lessons are hard-learned. Those with the highest of life's callings often seem destined to face life's greatest challenges. They can be besieged by failure and struggle, and are often viewed as damaged goods.

I would submit that in reality the opposite is true. That the struggles and failures such people endure are actually a signal that they are people who have chosen a higher calling. Within each of us is a calling higher than we can imagine. Purpose and challenge are, indeed, inextricably linked, forming the tangled web of life's experience. Those who choose to face the storm and walk through its fury find their highest purpose. Great heroes are thus forged. It is in our choice to engage the challenge that we come to acknowledge the value of the struggle—a struggle in which we are equipped to take hold of our destiny.

Here is where we come to find the "why" of why we are here.

ASSAULT ON OUR SELF CONFIDENCE

Times marked by conflict can bring with them the feeling that something is wrong with us. We may feel flawed, or damaged. But the truth is, conflict is part and parcel of the human experience.

I would like to share some valuable life lessons with you in this chapter. My intent is to help clarify these seemingly conflicting thoughts, to alleviate the confusion thrust upon us by circumstance and our pursuit of purpose.

In these hardest of times, we may find ourselves wandering around in what seems like fog. We are unable to get even a glimpse of where we are going. Knowing how to get there is completely out of the question. Where once the path was clear, we are now overcome by uncertainty. Doubt moves in, sets up shop, and launches an all-out assault on our self-confidence. The decisions which once seemed so right, now seem to be the very things leading us into this hard place. In the midst of it all, our self-esteem can take a battering.

To make things worse, circumstances come at us hard and fast. Feelings of doubt are joined by a sense of failure and hopelessness. People we once considered to be friends are now nowhere to be seen, and you can find yourself alone in the fight. The deal is that your friends are still your friends, but they cannot walk through this with you. It's your place, not theirs.

Fears flood our minds that our birthright has been squandered, and we lose hope that we will ever regain it. There seems to be no end to the malaise, and we are convinced that things will never be the same.

I have good news for you. The antidote for redeeming our self-confidence and self-esteem is to embrace our purpose and dedicate ourselves to the unfettered pursuit of it. If you choose to turn and confront the hard times, things will be better because you will be better. You will be wiser, you will be more seasoned, and better equipped to take on all that life has for you.

PURPOSE REVEALED

At the turn of the 20th century, Texas was a rural state where people raised cattle, cotton, and grain.[11] There were no large cities, and cotton was king. Galveston was one of the state's largest cities, a thriving port that sat on a barrier island which was little more than a sand bar standing just eight feet above sea level. With a population of thirty-six thousand, Galveston was known as the Wall Street of the Southwest. All was good.

Until it wasn't. Everything was about to change, and nothing would ever be the same. In the span of four months, Texans would learn the extent of Mother Nature's fury. And yet, amid the destruction, Texans would find provision for their purpose.

September 8, 1900, was indeed a dark and stormy night, a night that would signal a change in Texas forever. With little warning, a category four hurricane with one-hundred-forty mile-per-hour winds made landfall at Galveston, pushing a fifteen-foot storm surge which inundated the island. That fateful night, homes were turned to rubble by the relentless pounding of storm surf. Stories of the population's struggles to survive are the stuff of legend. The most poignant was about a group of nuns at an orphanage built by the shore. Thinking it best, they tied their children together so that none would be lost. However, ninety children and the nuns perished together in the relentless seas.

In the storm's wake was left a scene of chaos of destruction, with six to twelve-thousand people dead. As the citizens of Galveston began to dig out of the carnage, horrific scenes of death and devastation confronted them. Afterward, undaunted, they began to rebuild, determined to overcome this tragedy. Things were, however, never the same.

However, that is not the end of the story. It began with immense tragedy, but it ended in redemption.

Fundamental change was in the offing. Investors turned inland a full forty-five miles to build in Houston. A great harbor was created and a ship channel dug, stretching all the way to the Gulf. Houston's destiny and the future of Texas was no longer tied to cotton, or bound by the destruction of a hurricane. Something else was about to claim ascendency in the future of Texas.

Four months and two days after landfall of the hurricane, another event shook Texas to its core. On January 10, 1901, oil was discovered at Spindletop, a salt dome near Beaumont.[12]

That first well came in with such force that one-hundred-thousand barrels a day gushed out of it for nine days straight, before it was finally brought under control. Production from that single well doubled the total output of oil for the entire country.

Those nine days changed Texas forever. Texans began to drill for oil and seemed to strike it wherever they drilled. Refineries and petrochemical plants would spring up all along the coast, and many of our nation's largest oil companies would be birthed. Cotton was no longer king, oil was.

The state's high purpose was revealed in the aftermath of the chaos and destruction of Galveston's tragedy, and as a result, Texans were transformed into a people ready to take hold of their own future.

THE ACT OF TRANSFORMATION

Each of us is endowed with high purpose and the potential to be a person of influence. That purpose is not found by still waters or on a calm spring day. The person we are to become is molded in time of high stress and challenge. Character and courage are fashioned in the storm. Times of great challenge form the bounds of our integrity and test its strength. We quickly learn what price we are willing to pay for the principles we hold dear.

However, it is not what we learn that is the most important thing to happen to us in the midst of travail. Rather it is the kind of person we become. ***For in the midst of the storm, we are transformed into the person we need to be to accomplish the purpose for which we were created.***

There is pain to be endured, that is for certain. But it is as Garth Brooks said in his song *The Dance*, "I could have missed the pain, but I'd have had to miss the dance."[13]

Trust me on this, I've been there. You do *not* want to miss the dance.

How do we make sure that we don't go through all this pain only to find out we missed the transformation?

This takes us back to the battle for the mind, the choice we have talked about before (see Chapter 1). It is a binary choice and is controlled by an act of your will.

Your mind is an extremely powerful force. The process I'm about to describe takes place many times over the course of a life. Many of us experience it on a routine basis with varying degrees of intensity. In real terms, you are what you see yourself to be. The choices are not always clear, but they are conscious choices, to be sure.

VICTIMIZATION

Victimization is a life position that allows circumstances to reign over us and keep us in bondage to them. The world in which we live is not fair. It has never been fair, and it will never be fair. Creating an expectation of fairness only sets us up to live the life of a victim.

In its most severe form, the victim mindset leads one to believe that the cards have been stacked against them and they cannot succeed without the help of someone else. It is true that life is less fair to some of us than it is to others (see Chapter 1), but it is what we choose to do with it that counts.

The road to victimization is paved with unrealistic expectations of what life owes us. An example is in order here. My wife's father was an amazing musician. He had perfect pitch, meaning he could hear when a musical note was in tune or when it was not. He could play the trombone with the best of them and sang beautiful harmony. He was said to possess such an accurate ear for pitch that one could tune an entire band to the tone from his trombone. It was a gift he was born with, and he could easily have been a professional musician. On the other hand, me? Not so much. I'm pretty good at math and science, but I'm never going to write a great country song—it's just not in me. Pursuing music as my life's work would only lead to frustration, failure, and potentially life as a victim.

An alternate path is when we are tempted to take up the offense of someone else and make it our own. When I was a home builder, from time to time people would ask me for advice, which I was willing to give. A couple approached me at one of my open houses and asked me about a house they were thinking about buying. They told me all the wonderful things they liked about the house, that it was perfect for their family and how they really wanted to purchase it. Then they went on to tell me about the problems with the house, and it became apparent that it had significant foundation issues. My advice to them was to not buy that home. I explained that the current owner had a severe problem on his hands. If they were to buy it, they would be buying his problem and making it their own.

A decision to buy would have been an example of how an unwise choice can result in another's problem becoming your own.

We can extend this to the arena of the mind when we see someone in a hard place, or being treated unfairly by life. It is easy to let our compassion get out of control and lead us emotionally to buy into their problem. I don't know about you, but I have plenty of problems of my own without going out and gathering up the problems of others. These are times when we are engaged with other people, trying to help, but wind up taking their issues upon ourselves. It is not helpful to let our emotions get in the way of reason. You cannot help someone out of victimization by becoming a victim yourself, any more than your Doctor can help you get well by getting sick himself.

SOVEREIGNTY

Sovereignty is a lifestyle of choice where we choose to be victorious over our circumstances and assume our rightful place as the ruler of our lives. The life of a sovereign looks inward for the strength to achieve and live the life that he or she deems best.

Every one of us, regardless of our condition in life, has the power and the right to rule as sovereigns over our lives. Sovereignty is the sworn enemy of shame, blame, and victimization. Since this is such a critical concept, I would like to examine it further.

Sovereignty is a state of being where one has the ultimate authority and power, much like the rightful status of a king or queen. It applies to a nation whose people have the inalienable right to self-rule and to establish the form of government its people determine to be best. In a personal context, it applies to our life, how we think of ourselves, what we allow to happen to us, and how we choose to respond.

A good example can be seen when you go to the hospital and they ask you to sign documents giving them permission to treat you. They do this because you reign as the sovereign over your life and your authority is clearly set forth in our legal codes. Personal acts of sovereignty exist on multiple levels. The principles discussed here reside on the battle-field of the mind where our struggle for self-image, self-respect, inner health, and sense of accomplishment is waged.

The core competencies of sovereignty are inner strengths which are available to us all and enable us to live contented, productive lives.

- **Personal Responsibility** is the foundational competency upon which all others are based. It is the practice of establishing independence of thought and action. Taking personal responsibility means basing all our decisions on our own internal belief system and rejecting outside influences that would lead one to act in a way inconsistent with those values. Personal responsibility empowers one to own a problem and construct a healthy response regardless of the source of that problem. A person thus understands that neither the behavior of another nor the unfairness of a circumstance will assuage them of their responsibility to respond in a healthy, respectful manner.

- **Independence of thought** is when we reserve the right to think for ourselves and decide what is right and important, free of outside influence and the opinion of others. The power of "no" is an indispensable weapon at our disposal.

- **Emotional health** is critically important to our well-being. It is an area of our lives that needs to be nurtured as one would tend a highly manicured garden. Putting emotions in charge or allowing outside influences to determine how we feel is a fatal mistake. Our powers of clear thinking and self-control must remain sovereign over inner feelings, and stand guard against outside pressures that would harm us. Providing an inner protective envelope for our emotions allows them to function in a healthy manner.

- **Supremacy over circumstance** results from the sovereign power of choice. If properly deployed, it will lead to a victorious life, a life which takes on the obstacles in our path, turns us into overcomers, and empowers us in our purpose.

- **Ruling by principle** means establishing our principles as the final arbiters of our thinking. It is a conscious act that focuses our logic and decision making in a healthy direction. A life lived in accordance with sound principle brings blessings to us and all of those with whom we come into contact.

- **Power of the present** is accomplished by choosing to keep our thoughts focused on the now. Being present is essential to maintaining a healthy, well-adjusted life. Focusing on the past only sets us up to be depressed by things we can do nothing about. Focusing solely on the future opens us up to worrying about things that may never happen. Staying in the present keeps us in contact with what is truly important.

- **Personal boundaries** help us stay focused on the issues we are facing ourselves, and keep us from being distracted by the problems of others. Everyone has problems, it's a given. It becomes dysfunctional when we choose to take on the problems of others and make them our own. We each have a journey and a purpose, and it will take all our attention, energy, creativity, and focus to navigate our journey and fully realize our purpose. Establishing personal boundaries ensures that our resources are available for our pursuit of destiny.

The choice to live in the way described above is a conscious decision. These are sovereign acts of thought that protect our inner health and wellbeing.

SOVEREIGNTY IN SUPPORT OF PURPOSE

Let's examine how the concept of sovereignty supports the pursuit of purpose.

Think of sovereignty as a space that is created by you, along with how that space provides a secure place for you to live out your life as you choose. Think of a country that establishes its borders and declares that no hostile outsiders shall cross those borders or interfere with the activities of the people within those established boundaries. The borders and the freedoms of the people who live within them must be defended, and that's why nations have militaries. The strength of the national economy and the quality of life of a nation's citizens depend upon the successful exercise of national sovereignty.

Now let's think about your personal sovereignty and how you establish it through the power of choice, through the strength of your will. It is your will that defends the sovereignty of you against outside forces and unprovoked circumstance. This is the condition of free people, and of a free mind. With firmly established personal boundaries and a personal commitment to defending those boundaries comes the atmosphere in which you are free to accomplish all that you were designed to accomplish.

A STORY OF SOVEREIGN CHOICE

I think a story here would be helpful.

I had a major medical situation several months ago. It began with an uneasy feeling early one morning that escalated rapidly throughout the day. By three o'clock in the afternoon I was in the hospital contemplating the afterlife as a viable alternative to the stabbing pain I was experiencing. The doctor came in and told me he was scheduling surgery for that night, and I was dangerously close to finding myself in intensive care. I hurt so badly I told this complete stranger just to do whatever he needed to do.

Now, let's examine this. I was telling this man in a white coat that he could put me to sleep and cut into me, and I didn't know him from Adam. In retrospect, that sounds kind of crazy. I jokingly equated this to a guy who showed up at a knife fight only to fall asleep. In my moment of great need, I willingly surrendered my sovereignty to this man.

Following surgery, I spent the next two days lying in bed connected to tubes and monitors looking sick, acting sick, feeling sick, and the pain from the surgery wasn't getting much better. In a perverse way, I was enjoying all the attention. I was just plain pitiful. Then came the day when they removed the tubes, disconnected me from the machines, and told me that the more I got up and moved around the quicker I could go home. Now they were talking my language—I had a goal.

Here is one of those moments of choice I've been telling you about. I lay there in bed for a while thinking about this deal. I then made a fateful decision. I decided to quit acting like a sick person. I got out of bed, walked out to the nurse's station wearing that cute little blue number tied in the back, told them I was going to put on my clothes, and asked them if they had a problem with that. No, they didn't, but I was going to need some help putting on my socks and shoes. From that moment forward, I wore real clothes and sat in a chair rather than lying in bed. Things began to improve and the pain started to dissipate rapidly.

On my last day there, a lady from hospital administration came by to do an exit interview. When she walked into the room I was sitting there dressed like I was on my way to the gym. She looked at me and said, "Oh, I guess the patient isn't here." I informed her I **was** the patient. She said, "You don't look sick."

I grinned at her and said, "Exactly."

What just happened? I decided that my days as a victim were over, and I was going to rule again as sovereign in my life. I didn't think that I could change my physical condition, but I could change my response to it. Interestingly, when I changed my response to it, I did change my physical condition for the better. Hmmm, interesting.

The decision to control my response coupled with acting like I was sovereign literally changed my physical condition and the atmosphere around me. Did I have a long way to go? Yes, I did—I had a six-week recovery process. I was instructed what I could and could not do. Did I listen? Yes. Every good king listens to his advisers. That's called wisdom.

Here is what I want everyone to know. I'm nothing special, and I really don't know how I came up with this idea. I'm just like you. Draw your own conclusions.

Make your choice—victim or sovereign.

THE ROLE OF THE CULTURE OF FATHERHOOD

The role of a culture infused with the principles of fatherhood extends beyond the family and into our nation as a whole. Leadership is critical because people tend to follow their leaders.

A true leader is not one who seeks to be awarded with privilege, but rather, one who embraces an important set of responsibilities. A leader can bring peace and resolution, or they can choose to enflame. The latter is destructive, and leadership that trades in the currency of incendiary behavior should be called to account. Inflammatory leadership can lead to victimization. It fails to bring resolution and deepens problems by creating opponents rather than partners. This dynamic effectively blocks the path to the resolution their followers so desperately desire. For true resolution, we must turn to leaders who promote solutions that work, and help us along the path to personal sovereignty.

The father's role in the family is quite complex. It is important to understand that children imitate what they see, much more so than from doing what they're told. If we want our children to practice healthy behaviors, we will need to practice it ourselves, and do so in a way that they see. But here's the rub, we are innately imperfect beings. We make mistakes as we learn and grow, and our children will imitate those, as well. All you can do is get up every morning and confront life with the best that is in you.

Our children are also destined to face hard times. The challenge for a father is to know what to do to help them. The choice is not a binary one, but is very complicated. Do we wade in and rescue them? Or rather, do we let them struggle, suffer, and strive?

Our purpose is not to ensure our children's comfort. I believe our purpose is to see that they become all they can be. Overprotection will rob them of their chance to grow, and the opportunity to develop the skills they need to deal with adversity.

It is easy to understand that we need to let a child fall when learning to walk, or they will never learn that skill. It's more difficult when they are older and the stakes are so much greater. These decisions are tough. How much help is helpful? Will our help stunt their growth or rob them of the invaluable lesson that choices have consequences? What are the limits of their endurance?

These are the most difficult of all decisions. Parents must be committed to push and challenge. When your children are growing up, it is not the time to accept anything but their best, nor is it a place for the timid. If allowing them to learn means that extremely hard decisions need to be made, we must have the courage to do so. We must be prepared to let our children fail, and to let them endure, because those storms stand between who they are and who they can be.

Dealing with circumstance when it presses in upon us is an inevitable part of life. Our ability to deal with hardship looms large in our quest for happiness, contentment, and fulfillment. We have the opportunity to use those times to be transformed into the person we are meant to be and accomplish what we were designed to accomplish. A successful life is not defined by the absence of hardship but rather by our victory over it.

We have a choice to be victimized by traumatic events, or to claim our rightful position of sovereignty. Purpose may be found on the crumbling walls of an old mission, or in the aftermath of violent storms. Choosing to endure is the price of admission into your purpose, for it is endurance that qualifies you to be a person of influence.

CHAPTER 7 REVIEW QUESTIONS

1. What life experiences have the potential to bring about transformation and provision to help us fulfill our purpose?
2. What basic transformation happens inside us in the midst of a storm, that enables us to attain to our highest calling?
3. Compare the concepts of sovereignty and victimization, and how your life can be impacted by them.
4. Compare and contrast leadership styles that promote victimization with those that promote sovereignty.
5. What is the proper response to the storms that come into our lives?
6. Are there examples in your life where great challenges transformed you in a positive way? In a negative way?
7. What price are you willing to pay to walk into your purpose?
8. Rate yourself against the seven principles of sovereignty. Do you see any opportunities to strengthen yourself to live more victoriously?

CHAPTER 8

THE VALUE OF FAILURE

It is not the critic who counts; not the man who points out how the strong man stumbles, or where the doer of deeds could have done them better. The credit belongs to the man who is actually in the arena, whose face is marred by dust and sweat and blood; who strives valiantly; who errs, who comes short again and again, because there is no effort without error and shortcoming; but who does actually strive to do the deeds; who knows great enthusiasms, the great devotions; who spends himself in a worthy cause; who at the best knows in the end the triumph of high achievement, and who at the worst, if he fails, at least fails while daring greatly, so that his place shall never be with those cold and timid souls who neither know victory nor defeat.[14]
—Theodore Roosevelt

F ailure is not the ultimate defeat because there is no true defeat in it. Giving a person the freedom to fail is liberating, encouraging them to try new things that are beyond their reach. The entry into the place you were meant to possess is often found at the point of failure. In the midst of the pain, uncertainty, and insecurity lies a critical choice: Am I willing to take the risk again, or am I not?

The choice to turn back is perfectly reasonable and no one will fault you for it. However, the choice to try again reveals the gate through which you enter to achieve your goal and enjoy the fulfillment you deserve. Facing down failure and pressing through it creates the strength in us to meet the next challenge.

Our unique capacity to try, fail, and try again is an area of human nature that few of us want to embrace. It is a part of who we are that is difficult to appreciate until our travails are all over and we see how integral failure was to our growth. It has been said of a man that what happens to him today is what makes him the man he becomes tomorrow. We don't enjoy the experience, nor look forward to its return, but those things that test us most are the most necessary.

A healthier perspective is presented in the pages following. It is the perspective of a boy who admired the man who gave him life, a man who spent himself in a worthy cause.

TAKING THE STAGE OF GREATNESS

Failure holds a unique place in the human experience. It is not something to be feared, but rather embraced as part and parcel of our journey. Small failures often serve as teachers that help us avoid bigger problems in the future. Failure molds and forms the human spirit, preparing our character for our significant achievements to come. Many who have embraced their sovereignty and walked out onto the stage of greatness have done so amid the fog of failure.

Perfection as a goal is unattainable. It is an illusion, like the pot of gold at the end of a rainbow. Many have met with nothing but frustration and disappointment in the pursuit of it. The unachievable can be a hard taskmaster, leaving one broken and without hope of a future. Spending ourselves in the pursuit of perfection will leave us exhausted and often faced with the failings we fear the most. However, accepting our imperfections and spending ourselves in the pursuit of our sovereign purpose is a journey that culminates in a great sense of accomplishment.

Failure is a gift whose value is difficult to measure and nearly impossible to appreciate. You may be thinking, "What! Is this guy crazy?!" Some would say I am, but I assure you I am not. Failure and its first cousin, imperfection, are very good teachers. There have been many times they seemed like my constant companions. These were the times when I questioned my ability to do anything right. Times like these are when one's self esteem can take a real battering. But true greatness and high purpose can be discovered in the midst of perceived failure. It is where we gain strength.

An illustration is appropriate here. Think of when you start an exercise program and how sore you become. I am told that is because of micro-tears in your muscles. It takes a few days for the soreness to go away while those tears heal. Something theraputic happens in the process—your muscles get stronger. If you choose to exercise over and over again you will get progressively stronger. If you decide to avoid the soreness and stop working out, you will lose whatever gains you made. This is precisely what happens when we choose either to face failure or to avoid it.

As humans, we have a tremendous capacity to fail, learn, try again, and then succeed mightily. That process is rooted in our imperfect nature and is impossible to disentangle from our ability to learn and our drive to advance. It is as though important life lessons can only be achieved through failure, and that true riches are found in the time of our greatest need.

History abounds with examples. Edison, for instance, invented multiple ways *not* to invent a light bulb before he succeeded in actually inventing one. However, there is no better example than the life of Winston Churchill.

Churchill was a complicated figure, a man driven to leadership, who was not afraid to try and fail. During his military and political life, he had many successes and many failures. He bore the brunt of the blame for the disastrous Gallipoli Campaign in the First World War, and departed from government under a cloud of failure. It was a failure many never forgave.

But he rose again. He ascended in the early days of the Second World War to become Britain's Prime Minister, as the Allied forces of France and Britain stood on the precipice of defeat. He stood alone in Parliament and gave a speech that rallied the British people. He declared that they would fight wherever the battle took them, and affirmed, "We shall never surrender!" Those were the words of a man who stood on the precise place in history for which he was created.

The nation rallied to him. The people were emboldened. They rose and came together to save their country. It was the power of his oratory and the dauntlessness of his spirit that saved their nation. It took all he had, but he did not fail. The failures of his past had taught him all he needed to know, and prepared him well for this moment. Mr. Churchill certainly knew how to take the stage of greatness.

EMPOWERED TO EMBRACE FAILURE

How do we as a people prepare to embrace the lessons of failure? How do we come to appreciate the man in the arena "who spends himself in a worthy cause?"[14] More important, what causes us to strive to be the man who, "if he fails, at least fails while daring greatly?"[14] What is the essential element of character that sustains our self-esteem through the dark days, when we try mightily and fall with painful ferocity? What, amid failure, saves a man from destruction and compels him to carry on? What is it in the human experience that takes failure and turns it into character?

The answer for me is simple—love.

I'll bet you didn't see that one coming. Remember the story of my father? You know, the kid who learned to walk with one good leg. The man whose life was spent achieving that which many said was unachievable. It's guaranteed that he experienced many falls along the way. There were, surely, many times when he had to overcome the fear that gripped him as he pushed far beyond his limits. Somewhere in that struggle grew a character trait, a principle that defined him. My father showed me that real failure was not the fall itself but, rather, the failure to try. There was no place in him for the thought, "I can't walk because I have a crippled leg." There was something buried deep within him, the heart of a fighter that declared, "I have one good leg, and that's all I need." It was out of this strength of character that his sustaining principle found utterance in his signature statement, "Can't never could do anything."

Even so, he imparted something far more important—his love for me, a love that was never contingent on anything I did or didn't do. A love that he never withdrew when I fell, literally or symbolically. He would smile, pick me up, dust me off, and send me on my way. In the midst of failure, we need to learn to smile at ourselves and love ourselve, anyway. That small smile will lift your spirits.

THE CAPACITATING VALUE OF LOVE

In a culture driven by fatherhood, fathers are first and foremost charged with the creation of a safe place. Fathers are responsible for creating and maintaining environments where young ones can grow and learn to advance. The driving force behind their every action must be love.

It is love that sustains us through times of transformation. In times of turmoil, children may misunderstand and come to doubt your love, but you must never falter in giving it. For, the real purpose of your love is to instill in them a love for themselves.

In my darkest time, when the housing market and my poor business decisions were crumbling my business, I could see no way out. I told myself the most important thing was to remain true to that which I was. I committed myself never to change the person who had been molded by my father's love. The hard times changed a lot of things, but it never changed my character or caused me to sacrifice my integrity on the altar of expediency. His love had succeeded in equipping me to be the man who stayed true to his standards.

When our children fail, it presents a strategic opportunity to demonstrate the depth of our love and teach a great lesson. This is easy when they set a lofty goal and fall short. However, when they walk into disaster through poor decisions or the choice to follow bad friends, it becomes more difficult.

As our children move into adulthood, the stakes get higher and the consequences of failure loom more harshly. It seems much more difficult for young people to make the transition into adulthood today than it was in times past. Kids seem to have a limitless supply of poor choices at their disposal these days, and if they don't find them themselves, the internet stands ready to help. Young people can easily get into a downward spiral of poor decisions that conceive progressively more and more destructive choices.

Frustration then replaces the warm and fuzzy sense of love, in you and in them. In the frustration and despair of your child not making good choices, you may start to feel angry. You may hear yourself saying, "I didn't raise them that way." That may well be true. However, the reality is that you have a child in crisis, and there is not another you to help. The reality is that you, too, may not have any good choices at your disposal—only tough judgment calls.

Welcome to where the rubber meets the road of fatherhood.

So, what are you going to do in that situation? Understand this clearly: The choice of love calls for specific action.

You will be faced with the task of finding a way to act so your children understand that your love is still there for them. They need to know that your love is totally unconditional.

On top of that, you are tasked with finding a way to help without stunting their growth. We must give our children the freedom to fail, if we want them to become all they were meant to be.

At this critical juncture, a man needs a good woman. It's not a mystery that a child needs a mother as well as a father. It takes both to create a child, and it takes both to see them successfully through growing up. It is crucial that a man reach out to and listen to the woman in his life during these times, and lean on the supportive strength that only a woman's perspective and nature can provide. Your child needs both influences.

It's been said that behind every good man is a good woman.

As Yoda famously said, "Wrong thinking this is." Women are not meant to stand behind a man. Her rightful place is beside him, a coequal in sustaining their children as they navigate through troubled waters.

I would refer you back to Chapter 1, where my dad's mother and father stood together for him. She was her husband's rock when he began to falter, and they were an amazing team. Because of the sovereignty they claimed over their son's life, my dad's future was assured. They completed their mission-critical assignment because they were united in a common goal, each contributing his or her unique qualities and thus assuring that their youngest would live the life his disease had intended to steal.

VITAL ROLE OF MEN

Let me be very clear on this point, as it is an essential message of this book.

Men, your children need you. The nation needs you to step up.

Children learn from what they see, and they can't learn from you if they don't see you. The vital role a father plays cannot be reliably replicated.

Are there a lot of great kids being raised well by single mothers? The answer is most assuredly yes. Are there a lot of men living outside the home that are doing phenomenal jobs as dads? Absolutely yes.

But if the father is absent and the children are compelled to go looking for a substitute for the father they long for, who is that going to be? Is it going to be a man who demonstrates good, solid qualities? Are you willing to take that chance—a chance no better than the role of a dice? More important, do your children deserve more than that from you? I think they do. They deserve to have you there when they fail and fall, in order to give them the guidance of a father who encourages them to try again.

What if your situation isn't perfect? Suppose you don't have that special man or woman you desire to stand beside you. In the real world, there is no such thing as a perfect family. There are no families that meet all the standards of life described herein. In the spirit of full disclosure, my father was not perfect, and our family situation was not perfect. If my father were to read this work, he would tell me he didn't deserve such an honor.

In the real world, there are no fathers without fault. The good news is, whatever your circumstances, you have it in your DNA to fill the missing gap simply with your love. As a parent, you have an inalienable responsibility to raise your children and protect them from the life-altering pain of having an absent parent.

Be of good cheer and fill your heart with thankfulness that you have been entrusted with the special young people in your life. They are truly life's blessing.

CRITICAL CHOICES FOR PARENTS

Critical choices seem to be coming at us these days with greater frequency and ferocity than in the past. We must understand that the world our children deal with today is much more difficult than the simpler world we dealt with. The process of growing out of adolescence and into adulthood is markedly more difficult.

As my wife and I went through hard times with our children, we learned a lot. Much of it centered around what *not* to do. We found ourselves searching for something to help. Oftentimes, whatever it was it *didn't* help, and our plans hurt more than they helped. Many times, the right move was to do nothing.

Doing nothing is not particularly ingrained in my DNA. As I struggled to understand the situations I found myself in, it was easy to draw false conclusions about why my children were doing what they were doing, and about the quality of my parenting. I noticed times when their struggle only resulted in them sinking deeper. And there were times when their strengths turned upon them.

You will find yourself at critical junctures where you must decide whether or not to help your children through whatever it is they're dealing with. Will helping only serve to enable, or is your help truly what they need? Said another way, will jumping in to assist them help or thwart the learning experience of failure?

This decision is a tough one. When your children are at this crucial place and you are their only hope for guidance, what are you going to do? There are times when you must make the tough decision to let them walk it out alone. Then there are the times when you should throw them a lifeline. But how do you know which to choose?

You may want to consider the following:

- Are the probable consequences of your child's mistake a reasonable outcome? Or is life dishing out a disproportionate measure of punishment?
- If you fail to throw a lifeline, will the child go to a place that is so difficult he or she may not be able to recover?

- Is there a good lesson to be learned from this situation about actions and consequences?
- From what you know about your child, is this a genuine cry for help or one that will only lead to more bad choices?
- Is the child being treated unfairly, or the consequences what they truly deserve?

There are many more questions you can think to ask. My point here is that you as a father must think through this logically and park your impulses on the sidelines. Just remember, when in doubt, err on the side of compassion. Whatever may come, your children need to know you believe in them and that you see the best in them.

Interestingly, this is also true outside of the family. If we want to be good managers of people and great leaders of our nation, this is exactly how we need to think.

RELATIONAL BROKENNESS

Not one of us grows up without a violation of love and trust in our life. It's sad, but true.

Whenever people are in a dysfunctional lifestyle or living in perpetual hardship, there is always a story behind it. The brokenness of peoples' hearts is present today in near-epidemic proportions. Hearts are so often broken in childhood, and in many cases by the absence of a father. Our hearts are most severely broken by those with whom our relationships are closest.

People are damaged in school and in the workplace when they do not receive the reward they deserve, or must stand by and watch others get credit for what they accomplished. People everywhere are crying out. Many times, they just want someone to listen and understand them.

The thing most of us want is for someone to reach out and love us. We don't want to be fixed, nor do we want to be analyzed. We don't need everyone to weigh in with their favorite armchair psychology.

I know because I was there. Amid my great financial crisis, there were plenty of critics and people who wanted to fix me. But what I really needed was compassion and reassurance. I simply needed someone to love me. Eventually, I made it out of the malaise, but I did it alone. I was able to do that because I was raised by a man who demonstrated what it was never to give up, even when the worst life has to offer is thrown at you.

Let this be a call to arms for men of integrity and empathy everywhere to arise. Overcome whatever it is that life has used to beat you down. Stand straight and tall and strong. Look to your children and the children of others who are hurting. Reach out to them in compassion. Become the father that they need. Resolve in your heart to fill the father-shaped hole that is in theirs.

This is a call to embolden fatherhood in our culture, a call to reach out to the younger generations and firmly plant their feet on the path that will lead them to their greatness. If you are reading these words and wondering if I'm talking to you, quit wondering. I *am* talking to you and I challenge you to reach down deep into your inner well of manhood to do what is right.

You may have had no dad to teach you and show you. I assure you if you pay attention, you can find a good man for you to model yourself after. Fatherhood is written in your DNA. The right to practice it is inalienable, as is the responsibility it carries.

Failure is not to be feared, but rather embraced and accepted as a teacher. It is in failure we learn all that is required for us to take the stage of our greatest achievement. Failure holds a unique place in the human experience. The fear of it, not failure itself, is what grants it power over us. Love of ourselves is the best antidote to thwart that power.

CHAPTER 8 REVIEW QUESTIONS

1. What is the value of the gift of failure?

2. Have you encountered moments of failure in your life? What critical decisions have you been called to face?

3. In our families and our nation, what is the role of a father during critical times?

4. When you encounter a fellow traveler on the road of life whose circumstances are crumbling around him, what essential qualities of a father do they most need from you?

5. Which of the following statements is true: Failure is trying great things and falling short. Failure is the decision to not try at all.

Examine the times of failure in your life. Answer each of the following with absolute honesty. The answers will help identify the battlefield of the mind that you fight.

1. Are there areas in your life where you feel disqualified because of a personal failure in that area?

2. Are the failures of the past causing you to feel you are not as valuable as others?

3. Are there things you're passionate about that you're avoiding because of past failures?

4. Is failure preventing you from pursuing your purpose?

CHAPTER 9

CULTURE OF HONOR

And for the support of this Declaration, with firm reliance on
the protection of divine Providence, we mutually pledge to each
other our Lives, our Fortunes, and our sacred Honor.[15]
—Thomas Jefferson, Philadelphia 1776

If men are to be empowered through a culture that embraces the principles of fatherhood, then these concepts must extend far beyond the family and the raising of children. This is far more than a family issue. It is something that goes straight to the heart of a civilization's health and vitality. The words of fatherhood must infuse the voices of men of influence in every sector of our civilization.

Imagine if you will, what kind of world it would be if every man who is a politician, judge, businessman, or educator thought with the wisdom of a father and drew upon its principles to direct them. Let me use the political arena to explain what I mean by that.

Suppose we lived in a world where every politician espoused the same beliefs when his party was out of power as he did when his party was in power. Suppose we had legislators who voted solely based on what was good for the country, not what was good for their party or themselves. Suppose our leaders categorically rejected the idea that they would rather have the issue than the solution.

Suppose every political decision was driven by a father's heart whose aim was to provide, protect, and sustain our nation. I believe that would result in a country which is a measurably better place to live than what we have today. What could we become if all of our leaders simply spoke the truth, and what is true today is also true tomorrow?

SACRED HONOR

What if our leaders today thought like the men who gathered in Philadelphia in June of 1776? Our Founding Fathers gathered there to sign the Declaration putting forth that ours was a free and independent nation, a declaration that established this country as a sovereign nation. In so doing those men were committing high treason against King George. The last line right above their signatures reads as follows:

"And for the support of this Declaration, with firm reliance on the protection of divine Providence, we mutually pledge to each other our Lives, our Fortunes, and our sacred Honor."[15]

The signers of this pledge were soon to have the consequences of their pledge visited upon them.

These fifty-six men who signed the Declaration of Independence are now known as the Fathers of our Country. No better understanding of what I mean by Fatherhood can be expressed than by what they did.

Turn your attention to the final phrase, "our sacred Honor."[15] There it is—their honor was how they chose to describe the essence of the men they were, and honor was so important they considered it sacred. Honor was the core value by which each man chose to govern himself, thus qualifying him to be a true father of the new nation. Honor is also required at the core of men today who want to lead our country.

We don't have a crisis in political ideology—we have a crisis of honor.

ESSENCE OF HONOR

An understanding of the concept of what constitutes an honorable man is fundamental to the understanding of what is necessary for men to become men of influence as well as true fathers.

Raymond Chandler said that to such a man, honor is instinctual and inevitable.[8] Honor is not something one strives to achieve, like a badge or certificate. Honor is not something that can be attained by setting a goal and working toward it. Honor is something that resides deep within the soul of a man. Honor is not what a man does, it is what he is.

However, honor is not an all or nothing thing. We are all complex, imperfect people. Becoming a man of honor is a lifelong pursuit that is probably never completely perfected. In fact, if we ever stop and say we have arrived, we are in danger of losing it. Maintaining a position of humility is vital. The pursuit of honor is a process in which we seek to become a more honorable man tomorrow than we are today.

A man of honor, according to Chandler, is a man who walks the mean streets who is not mean nor afraid.[8]

The question is, from what is honor created?

Honor resides deep in a man's gut. True honor cannot be denied once it infuses a man's soul. Honor is the essence of who a man is, and is that which drives him. He holds it sacred and will protect it with everything he has and everything he is, even his life and his fortune. If he fails to heed its call, he will soon feel sickened and long remember those times when he violated the metes and bounds of honor in his heart. When, many years later, his thoughts return to those failures, he will be saddened by what he did and will be driven to never again violate his honor.

Honor is a quality that envelopes a man's heart and will guide him back to that which is right when he begins to wander. Honor runs in the background, and men who have it obey it without conscious thought. It's always with them, an essential part of them.

Honorable decisions often emerge with little conscious thought as to the basis for them. Make no mistake, if you choose a life of honor, it will rule the essence of you and become your primary reason for what you do.

An illustration is in order here to help better illustrate how honor works.

Honor is like electricity. When we go into a room and turn on a light, it automatically comes on without us thinking about the electrical power being sent to it. The power is always there. If we flip the switch and the light does not come on, we automatically assume that the bulb has burned out.

During Hurricane Harvey, we lost power overnight at our home in Houston. The next morning, we got up and the lights wouldn't come on. My thought process went like this:

> Light bulb burned out
> All the light bulbs burned out
> That cant be
> Breakers must have thrown
> All the breakers must have thrown
> Breakers are ok
> Oh my, no power
> Oh my, there is a hurricane in the Gulf

Honor is like that. It is the last thing thought of because it is always there. It is that which powers a man who embraces it. It is his first in-stinct. If he were to lose it, he would sink into incapacity.

There is, however, a necessary quality of soil required for the seeds of honor to take root and grow in a person. These are the core qualities of character, integrity, morality and competence, which we will explore in the following chapter.

CHAPTER 9 REVIEW QUESTIONS

1. What quality did the signers of the Declaration of Independence consider to be sacred? What is the significance of this?

2. Where does honor reside in a man, and how does a man of honor view it?

3. What is the core value a man must possess in order to father a legacy?

4. Assess your automatic responses to various circumstances and events. How do your reactions line up with the concept of honor?

CHAPTER 10

FOUNDATIONAL PILLARS OF HONOR

The ultimate measure of a man is not where he stands in moments of
comfort, but where he stands at times of challenge and controversy.[16]
— *Dr. Martin Luther King Jr*

Character, Integrity, Morality, and Competence.

Those are the pillars that underpin a culture of honor. These human qualities are available to all people through conscious choice. They are not hidden away in our minds but reside in our spirits. And these qualities are yearning to be freed. They are not something that one has to search for, but rather they are just waiting to burst forth from all of us. We must expend effort to hold them back. That is because these qualities reside at the inborn core of the goodness of the human soul.

Dr. King's words ring in the heart of a man of honor.

CHARACTER

Character is a measure of the quality of a man.

As a homebuilder, I thought of construction quality overall as the quality standards which a tradesman adhered to combined with the quality of materials which we used. A man's quality is much the same. It speaks to how well a man is built, and to what standards of construction.

As we go through life, we make hundreds of thousands of choices. It is in these choices that we mold the quality of who we are and what we become. For example, when you decide how to treat someone, are you going to decide to treat them fairly? Or will you take advantage of them? This kind of choice happens repeatedly throughout our lives, and little by little, our character is formed, good or bad, until our responses become automatic. The decisions we make during our life are the quality standards by which our character is constructed.

The good news is, we can always remodel our house and correct any shortcomings we find. A word of warning here though. Character flaws are very difficult to correct because they, by their very nature, deny that they exist. Protecting your character is something that requires vigilance and an unselfish devotion to high standards of conduct.

A man of character is a highly principled person with a finely tuned sense of responsibility which governs him at all times. Our character muscles are exercised when we are called to act. The most critical tests happen when we are under great stress, when the stakes are the highest, when the right decisions are not clear, and when the consequence of a bad decision is most severe.

Below are the types of things that a man of character will consider when faced with difficult choices.

- **Is it the right thing to do?** This is the "go-to" question. When all else fails an honorable man, the right thing is precisely where he will turn.
- **What does this say about who I am?** When the dust settles, am I going to be proud of myself for what I did and, more important, are those people most important to me going to be proud of me?

- **How does this decision affect the other person?** There are a lot of times when an honorable decision comes at a cost. You may be driven to a choice that is unfair to you but looks after another person. You can survive it. You may be called upon to make a decision based not on an agreement, but upon the greater need of another.

- **What is my responsibility in the matter?** A man of high character is invariably one with a well-developed sense of responsibility and a healthy view of it.

- **What is my purpose?** A man's true purpose in life is found in what he is passionate about and in that which drives him. A clear understanding of why you were made is an essential guidepost in life's journey. Devotion to its pursuit is an integral part of your character.

INTEGRITY

Living with integrity is central to the concept of honor. Integrity is a complex idea composed of three facets—truthfulness, honesty, and dependability. Integrity is not always easy, and often comes at a price. There are times when one must decide to act simply because it is the right thing to do.

An honorable man is a man who can be depended upon always to tell the truth. It's not hard for him, it is instinctive. To a man of integrity, it never occurs to him to be any different. To him, what is true today remains true tomorrow, for truth that changes is no truth at all. Truth that is fluid is merely a convenience to get what one wants. The man who commits his life to the practice of truth is one who is comfortable with all the consequences. These are men who are comfortable in their own skins. They like themselves as they are, and are unwilling to sacrifice honor for personal gain or comfort.

There is, however, more to integrity than a simple dedication to truth. Truth is, to be sure, the foundation for integrity, but integrity goes so much deeper.

It has been said that integrity is what a man does when no one else is watching. It is also what one decides when that decision's consequences are harsh. Integrity combines truthfulness with honesty.

Integrity defines a man's business relationships and his ethics in the workplace. A man of integrity is dependable. He can be counted upon to fulfill his obligations. To a man of integrity, the spirit of an agreement is as important as the letter and law of it. When wrestling with a decision concerning an agreement with another person, he asks himself what the other party understood the agreement to mean.

It all comes down to the concept that an honorable man will take nothing that isn't his, nor countenance those who do.

There is a third element to integrity, and it is one that many would not immediately think of—dependability. In the American West, we say that a man is as good as his word. When it comes to dependability, this takes on a very specific meaning. It means that when a person of honor tells you they are going to do something, they will do it, and there will be no equivocation. Such people don't need contracts or laws to force them to do as agreed. To a man governed by integrity, a contract is only needed as a written record of what they agreed to. They will do as they say, simply because they said they would. It's no more complicated than that.

MORALITY

Morality is the system of rights and wrongs, good and bad behaviors, and ethics that society adopts to govern itself. It is the code by which we, as civilized beings, restrain our inner demons.

The strength of a civilization depends upon its morality. Indeed, many of history's great civilizations fell because rampant immorality beset their societies.

The war for the souls of men is waged upon the battlefield of morality, for in each of us resides the capacity for good and the capacity for evil. Morality is that which restrains evil as defined by our society.

In the final analysis, the quality of a nation depends on its moral values and boundaries in order to thrive. In the aftermath of the attacks on Pearl Harbor, millions of young Americans joined our Armed Forces to right a wrong against our country. Their drive and the drive of countless servicemen and women since then comes from the moral fiber of this nation. How else to explain a young American soldier storming the beaches at Normandy to put a stop to the carnage on the European continent? The answer is that these were men of honor, driven by a moral code.

However, it goes deeper than that. The moral character of a society and that of the men I am trying to reach is in large part defined by how that society and those men protect the weak. There are real, serious problems which we as a nation need to address if the American civilization is to thrive.

I'm calling on men of honor to step forward to protect the weak. Systemic racism remains a stain on our national honor that is begging for honorable men to step forward and resolve the injustice. I personally believe that our failure to protect the unborn is a failure of our moral fabric. The same is true for people who are sold into slavery for the physical pleasure of others.

We, as a people, are honor bound to find solutions. The healing of these deeply hurtful wounds is something that eludes the capacity of government to resolve. That is because we are dealing with human behavior and that can only be changed by getting at one's core values. There is a lot of really good work being done at the grassroots level. The heart of honorable fatherhood is desperately needed to heal the wounds and to get at the root causes. The hope that we will ever see a complete eradication of these issues may seem like an impossible task. Sounds like that is right up our alley.

COMPETENCE

The last component of an honorable man is competence. It is not something we talk about a lot, but rather something we subconsciously think of when we are dealing with a person. It is the quality in a person that draws people to them when there is serious work to be done. If we want to be people of influence, then we must strive to be proficient in all the following areas.

PERSONAL COMPETENCE

Personal competence is an inner state of being with a deeply engrained skill set. It forms the foundation upon which professional and financial competence are built. This speaks directly to a man's ability to successfully navigate through life, and is marked by a natural self-confidence. It is also wrapped up in a man's purpose, as this is where our inner selves are provisioned. A man's skill is independent of his profession or his education.

I have known many young men in the construction business who had no college education, and some had even dropped out of high school. I've had conversations where I took the time to listen and learn. In many of these talks, I've been privileged to discover a rich understanding of life and a deep-seated wisdom in these men.

Personal competence is the space where the competence of fatherhood resides. Personal competence is derived from a man's inner self-awareness, strength, judgment, self-control, and wisdom. The quality of personal competence is desperately needed in every area of our lives, to resolve the problems that seem to be unresolvable.

Remember Billy Ray and how he relished the challenge of conquering the impossible, and went on to do it? That is what I mean by personal competence.

PROFESSIONAL COMPETENCE

A man of honor finds his place and his profession. The profession one chooses is far less important than the competence with which one approaches it. A professionally competent person takes pride in whatever job he chooses, and is driven by his character to do it well.

In the process of building custom homes, I worked with engineers and architects, bankers and attorneys, all professionally degreed people. But I also worked with the men who poured the concrete or framed the house, manual labor that required great skill. Although those men didn't learn their craft in a university, their work was no less competent than those with degrees.

The deal is this—without these tradesmen and their colleagues, we would have no homes. All work is honorable, and good men are needed to do it. If a man chooses to pursue a life of honor and competence, he must find his profession and do his work well.

FINANCIAL COMPETENCE

The ability to earn a good living and effectively manage financial resources is a critical life skill that puts a person in the position of being a good provider. It is a position that garners respect and makes a person independent.

Professional competence produces the income. Financial competence is the ability to manage it. A competent person will set aside some money in a separate account for future needs, and an honorable one will earmark a portion of his income for charity. Following that, he will establish a budget to control where his money is spent.

It's the concept of telling your money where to go, not watching it go out the door, that results in financial competence. Managing money in this way puts a person in a position to enjoy the fruits of his labors.

Character, integrity, morality, and competence are the pillars that underpin a culture of honor. These are the truly essential qualities that constitute the best of the human experience. Men with these qualities are what we need—good and honest men dedicated to always doing what is right, who cultivate a highly developed skill set of personal, professional, and financial competence.

Our desperate need today is for men of honor to step forward, bringing integrity-driven fatherhood to bear upon the seemingly impossible. I think by now we all understand the power of ethically-driven men—and women—who take on the impossible, and persevere until they overcome all obstacles.

CHAPTER 10 REVIEW QUESTIONS

1. What are the pillars of honor?

2. Define what character means to you, and how your life experiences have formed your character.

3. Assess your sense of personal responsibility and your commitment to act according to it.

4. What are the three elements of integrity, and how are these manifest in you?

5. What roles can men who possess strong moral codes play in resolving the stains on our nation's character?

6. What do the terms "personal competence" and "professional competence" mean to you?

7. Being honest with yourself, how do you measure up when you measure yourself by the four pillars?

8. What is your plan for growth in the culture of honor?

CHAPTER 11

END OF OUR TALE

There is meaning in every journey that is unknown to the traveler.[17]
— *Dietrich Bonhoeffer*

W̲e began our tale with the story of a man and his son on a wind-swept East Texas Lake. We learned of the father and mother who sustained him, set his feet on the ground, and willed him to walk. They spoke for him when he couldn't speak for himself. I would like to finish our tale with another story of that man and an event that speaks volumes about who he chose to become.

It was during the years of WWII. My mother and father were dating then, and had a close group of friends of about the same age. They worked in a Gulf Coast chemical plant supporting the war effort. They were members of the generation that grew into adulthood during the Great Depression and were fighting to win mankind's most destructive and lethal war. During WWII everything was rationed while the nation fully dedicated itself to the defeat of tyranny.

Late one night, my dad got a call from a friend who was coming back into town with his family, fresh from a visit to his hometown. They were stranded on the highway with a flat tire and no spare. The man made his way to a phone and called my dad for help.

Years later, he came by our house on the day of my dad's funeral, and told my brother and me this story. He said when he got to the phone, there was no question about who he would call. It was entirely natural to call Billy Ray. It was just so normal. He knew Billy Ray would answer, he knew he would come, he knew Billy Ray would show up with his tools, and most important, he knew that Billy Ray would know what to do when he got there. He and his family were in need, and they needed a dependable man. He needed a man who loved to help and had the competence to do so.

In many ways, we as a people are stranded on the highway of history and need dependable men to show up. There are three specific areas where highly competent men are needed to address long-standing problems in our country.

THROW AWAY PEOPLE

First, are the "throw-away" people. As an example, consider an angry young man in a riot who is arrested for destroying another's property. He has broken a law and the penalties of law should be enforced. Above all at this moment, he needs to learn that actions have consequences and they cannot be avoided.

The question is, then what are we to do with him? Are we to simply send him into the criminal justice system to be forgotten and labeled as a criminal—i.e. thrown away? What happens when he gets out? To be thrown away is incredibly unjust, and the continuance of this practice will only beget more anger and violence. The alternative is for us to be fathers and look deep into his soul, see the pain, and fill the father-shaped hole that is almost surely to be found there. If we are to succeed, fathers must engage him on a personal basis and help him to take responsibility for his life. That is, to infuse the spirit of sovereignty into him. There are a lot of good men and women going into the prisons and engaging the people there. You might want to join them.

THE TANGLED WEB OF FAULT

Second, is the tangled web of fault. There are issues in our land that are stains on our national character—they separate us rather than unite us, and the resultant polarization blocks any hope of resolution. These issues exist in the arena of political discourse and also in our family relationships.

Some issues date back to a time so long ago no one truly remembers how the anger or discord started or who started it. Consequently, we can find ourselves in a seemingly endless cycle of blame and recrimination. The understanding of healthy fathers is needed to step in and help break this continuous cycle. The solution will never be found in a process that labels the other side as evil. Doing so will only serve to turn the very people you need to partner with into your opponents.

Thinking that we need to vilify an entire class of people in order to address the injustices of a different aggrieved class will only ensure that the injustice is never rectified. Tenaciously clinging to the past and its injustices serves only to keep us entangled in the vain pursuit of something we can do nothing about, and deter us from real progress. The only solution lies in stepping up to take ownership of the present, forgiving the past, and focusing on solutions for the future.

This is not an argument for any one ideology, but rather a plea for solutions that actually work. Does it really do any good to convince everyone how evil an entire class of people is because of the indefensible actions of a few? I think not. I believe it is a fundamental mistake to inject our most devastating problems into the political arena. We may find allies there, but the capability of any political system to modify human behavior is very limited. There is pain emanating from deep wounds, to be sure. But, these are wounds that only people can heal. We would be much better served to sit down at the dinner table, look each other in the eye, and join together to find solutions.

SEXUAL ABUSE

Third, there is sexual abuse. There is no more devastating a problem, nor one which cries louder to cultural fatherhood for a solution than the problem of sexual abuse. It is a direct assault on a person's sovereignty that deliberately seeks to destroy their personal boundaries, thus leaving them in a vulnerable position that is defenseless against the next attack.

I can think of no worse thing than the sexual abuse of a child, or enslaving a person for sexual purposes, AKA human trafficking. Sexual abuse infests every sector of our society and is a much bigger, more persuasive problem than most of us realize. It is a malady that entraps its victims in shame and self-incrimination when they have done nothing wrong. The entrapment only makes them more vulnerable and steals the joy of healthy sexual relationships. If you are someone who has been abused there are resources available to you. I would refer you to the National Sexual Abuse Hotline 1-800-656-4673.

Sexual assault is an existential threat to the very soul of our people. It is self-propagating, as it operates in the shadows and hides from normal solutions. Fighting it is more like guerrilla warfare. We must become much more vigilant. This perverted behavior can be happening right around us and we may not know it. The competency of authentic fatherhood and the penetrating vigilance of parents is desperately needed in this battle.

PATH TO RESOLUTION

If we truly want resolution, there are three principles of problem solving that need to be applied here, and that can only be deployed from a reasoned and wise mind.

- We must give up the idea that the solution solely lies in identifying the group that is responsible for creating the problem and getting them to accept the blame for it. A related dysfunctional practice is presenting an exaggerated version of the issue to gain a tactical advantage. These practices lead to polarization, and will stand to block a solution, because they create enemies rather than partners. As Rocky said to Bullwinkle, "That trick never works."

- Every person must understand that he alone is responsible for his own actions, and nothing anyone else does will assuage him of that responsibility. Workable responses are those that target a solution and emanates from our personal, internal standards.

- Self-control and focus are important attributes one finds in true problem solvers. The ability of a man to control his emotions, operate in the present, and rise above the conflict equips him to lead the drive to workable solutions. True resolution is found when we pointedly address the root causes rather than the effects.

Fathers of integrity, we need you, the nation needs you. Men of honor are needed everywhere, in every city and town of our nation. We need you in the richest and the poorest of our neighborhoods, in the darkest of slums and the brightest of homes. We need you in the seats of government, on the most powerful judicial benches, and at the head of our great corporations. We need you on our construction sites and in our factories. We need you in every nook and cranny of this phenomenal country. We desperately need men who will answer, men who will come forward, men who are prepared, and men who will know what to do when they get there.

Men of honor who can lead us are in demand. These are the men who can empower us all to fulfill our highest purposes, to be the light that the world so desperately needs.

You may be asking yourself this question: the need for fathers is so huge and I am only one person. What can I do?

Well, I can't resist the desire to tell you one last story. There was once a 10-year-old boy walking along a beach. A storm the night before had washed up thousands of starfish on the beach, where they now lay dying.

The boy was walking along picking up starfish and throwing them back in the water. A man came along and asked him what he was doing. "Saving starfish," the boy replied. The man looked at the boy and said, "You can't make a difference. There are thousands of starfish." The little boy looked up at him with a smirk on his face and a twinkle in his eye, reached down, picked up a starfish, and threw it back in the water. He looked up at the man, grinned, and said, "Made a difference for that one."

If we pay attention every day, each one of us can make a difference in the life of one of our fellow travelers. To all men everywhere, I want you to know that you have what it takes. No matter where you are, how you were raised, or what you have done, you *can* be a man of honor. It is within you. It's written in your DNA. Everything you need is within your reach, if only you believe and determine in your heart that you will not give up on yourself. If you answer the call and reach out with a hand of fatherhood, you will see great things happen.

And then, maybe then, we will fight the final, long battle of the American Revolution. Maybe then we will finally secure liberty for all, unlock the creative power of all our people, and be a genuine light to the whole world.

Understand that, regardless of where you come from or your station in life, your contribution is indispensable. Your unique talents and placement in life cannot be replicated, and that makes *you* the only choice for the people you touch. The solutions to the issues facing us must come from among us. There is no one else who can fill your place. There is no one else who can influence the same people and decisions that you can, in the way that you can. No one else can impact *your* world for good as well as you can.

We have great challenges ahead of us, and ordinary men like you and me are compelled by force of honor to meet them.

Draw inspiration from the words of Admiral Halsey who said, "There are no great men, there are only great challenges that ordinary men are forced by circumstances to meet."[6]

If you answer the call and reach out with a hand of friendship and fatherhood, you will see great things happen and experience the true joy of helping your fellow travelers along their way.

Now I come to the end of my tale, one that began on a dark and stormy night in a small Texas town on the Gulf Coast where two very young parents made an incredibly brave choice. Theirs was a choice to speak for someone who could not speak for himself. Theirs was a choice that continues to ring down through the generations, even today, for without it I would not have been here to write this book. If there is anything in these pages that has touched your heart or made you a better person, you have them to thank.

What, now, is the story *you* are going to write? Every day you face challenges just as they did. And you get to write your own story by living the kind of life you choose.

Have fun, enjoy the journey, and let me know how it turns out.

CHAPTER 11 REVIEW QUESTIONS

1. What four qualities are needed in men and women to address society's most serious issues?

2. Three critical needs exist in our nation, a) the restoration of the "throw away" people, b) the untangling of the web of anger and blame, and 3) protection of the abused. What qualities of fatherhood can be used to address these?

3. Each of us is wonderfully designed to impact his or her part of society. What is your unique place?

4. Understanding that we are all works in progress, what areas do you need to grow within yourself in order to take your unique place in society?

THE CORE PRINCIPLES

CHAPTER 1—SOVEREIGNTY OF CHOICE

- Realism and determination are the drivers to see you through crisis.
- Crisis challenges your position of sovereignty.
- The principle of right and wrong is the life position that enables us to make decisions based on rightness, and the one that sustains us through struggle.
- A strategically placed "no" leaves no doubt as to who is going to reign as sovereign.
- The culture of fatherhood provides the place from which choice and resiliency draws its strength.
- Life's toughest challenges are effectively confronted by the following personal qualities:
- Absolute determination to always confront obstacles in your path.
- Strength of character to prevail no matter the cost.
- "I can't" and "I quit" are the enemies of choice and sovereignty.
- The expectation of fairness can lead to defeat and prolonged entrapment in self-pity.
- Asking why will entice us to adopt the life view of a victim.
- Taking personal responsibility for ourselves empowers us to overcome the inherent unfairness of life.

- The fundamental choice is your decision to control your life or let circumstances do it for you.
- In the arena of your purpose, you have the authority to make these fundamental choices and support them with the weight of a sovereign.

CHAPTER 2—DARK NIGHT ON STRIKER CREEK

- The quality of a person is measured by his self-governing commitment to do what he said he would do simply because he said he would do it.
- The health of our society, its system of justice, and its commercial transactions are based on its people adhering to the intent of an agreement as well as the letter of the agreement.
- The diligent pursuit of truth makes one trustworthy and contributes to a healthy self-image.
- Trustworthy people are given the benefit of the doubt when they are wrong, and that is a measure of healthy relationships.
- Truth's unalterable nature must be held sacred to sustain security, growth, and creativity.
- Truth is the unchangeable guidepost that leads us into safe harbor in time of trouble.
- Dedication to truth gives us the confidence to meet life's greatest challenges head on.
- An environment of truth is where men and women become all that they can be.
- Unquestioned dedication to right and wrong forms a man's character and earns him respect.
- Modeling life positions rooted in the principle of right and wrong is an essential role of fathers.
- A healthy culture of fatherhood challenges boys to become men and girls to become women.

- Men and women of character will do what's right regardless of the cost.
- Truth is true and not subject to the whims of circumstance.

CHAPTER 3—STANDARDS

- Change is inevitable and is necessary for us to grow as a nation.
- Unbridled change carries with it a danger that we must be vigilant to guard against.
- Embracing reasoned change is essential to the growth and maturity of the nation.
- Guarding against unintended consequences and judging the wisdom of making a change is the role of standards.
- Standards are like a lighthouse, a fixed point of navigation guiding us through troubled times.
- Our hallmark standards are fidelity, faithfulness, loyalty, responsibility, courage, commitment, devotion to service, and dedication.
- Relying on our inner belief system rather than external influences is a stabilizing quality of the human spirit.
- Compelling principles are like the light from a lighthouse unaffected by wind and rain.
- The light that emanates from our principles illuminates that which is right, true, just, and fair.
- Life's important decisions are best made when measured against consistent standards.
- Success comes from staring down life's challenges and giving back more than you receive.
- Overcoming those things which "cannot be overcome" is something to be cherished and enjoyed.
- In each of us is a core value that defines our true self.

- Discovering your true self and your core values is the process of personal discovery which focuses on what is important and identifies the things you are passionate about.
- Embracing and nurturing your true self will transform you into a person of influence.
- Four essential principles that define masculinity are:
- No possible outcome or personal agenda is righteous enough to justify trampling on the rights or feelings of others, or violating your true self.
- Vacating your responsibility is never justified by the inappropriate behavior of others.
- A higher level of responsibility is required of those who have been endowed with greater portions of wealth, power, and influence.
- Real progress happens when we objectively look at the facts as they are, and dedicate ourselves to finding solutions that work.
- True masculinity embraces these principles of high standards.

CHAPTER 4—IN SEARCH OF DESTINY

- Our ultimate purpose in life is often not what we originally thought it to be. In fact, it is often something we never dreamed of doing.
- Discovering the purpose for which we were born represents the second greatest day of our life, according to Mark Twain.
- Life's greatest adventure is the discovery and pursuit of our highest purpose. We often find the resources we need for our calling about the time we discover what our purpose is.
- Discovery of purpose is not found in a safe place, but rather when we risk leaving our comfort zone and journey into the unknown.
- Contentment and fulfillment reside in the adventure, and make the journey worth taking.

- The journey to purpose is resourced by the drive to engage and a determination to persevere.
- Success is dependent on the willingness to take on that which is difficult, along with the absolute determination to persevere regardless of the personal cost.
- Unshackling a person's spirit from the constraints of circumstance unleashes destiny's power.
- The best within us is found when we leave our comfort zone and pursue our highest purpose.
- Life's highest purpose is found when we face down that which we fear the most.
- Experiencing pain and hurt are essential elements in the pursuit of purpose.
- Nothing compares to the sense of accomplishment found when you stand on your mountain and realize what it was all about.

CHAPTER 5—THE MEASURE OF A MAN

- Taking on the essential positive nature of manhood is critical to the empowering of fathers and the sustenance of our culture.
- Overlaying healthy principles of masculinity with the heart of a father is a potent partnership.
- Authentic men are those who live by a set of beliefs based on sound fundamentals and who temper their power accordingly, enabling calm, reasoned decision making.
- The key qualities of manhood are: inner strength, authenticity, objectivity, resolve, propriety, courage, understanding, and wisdom.
- Manhood is marked by assertiveness, mental toughness, and an innate drive for respect. The drive for respect is so strong that a man will fight for it.

- Men are driven to provide, and gain a great deal of self-respect from doing so.

- Men are called to confront the mean streets without being tarnished by meanness. They will instinctively turn to confront danger if it threatens their people.

- More and more children are being raised in an environment where no healthy man resides. This is producing far too many broken boys and girls.

- Many of society's most troubling problems can be tracked to the absence of fathers.

- Inappropriate exercise of personal, financial, or positional power is not the mark of a man, but is rather the antithesis of true masculinity.

- True manhood means never putting oneself into a place of superiority or roughly exercising one's authority for selfish purposes, or for any purpose.

- Personal, occupational, and financial competence are qualities of authentic men.

- A real man clearly understands what is right or wrong, and more important, has the practiced will to temper his behavior to conform to those principles.

CHAPTER 6—PROTECTION, PROVISION, PERSEVERANCE

- The health of a society depends upon a system of mutually shared values.

- The growth and stability of a society depends on maintaining a critical mass of people dedicated to having a value-based society.

- Healthy fatherhood is an essential element of those values.

- Central to the concept of fatherhood is the drive to protect, which is derived from and empowered by a father's self-respect.

- Fathers own the ultimate responsibility to provide for the basics of life—food, clothing, transportation, and housing for the family.
- Life is not a straight-line journey but more akin to walking through a maze.
- Perseverance is that which sustains us in this journey and nurtures us in our quest.
- Perseverance keeps us on course and helps us to avoid the detrimental effects of unintended consequence.
- Traditions sustain our identities both as a nation and as families.
- Traditions bind us together and remind us there is more that unites us than divides us.
- Sustaining the nation's culture is critical, and is fueled by unselfish devotion to the common good, encompassed by the principles of protection, provision, and perseverance

CHAPTER 7—TRANSFORMATION IN THE STORM

- The existential struggle of the human experience is the unrelenting journey through life's critical experiences.
- Our journey to purpose passes through high stress times during which our ability to endure is tested, and often the greatest of life's lessons are learned.
- In each of us is a purpose that is realized when we embrace the storm, turn and face the challenge, and walk through its fury to find our high calling.
- In the hardest of times, we find ourselves wandering around in what may seem like a fog with no clear path before us, and feeling that our birthright has been squandered.
- Decisions that once seemed right can be the very things that lead us into the hard places where doubt launches an all-out assault on our self-confidence.

- The path to redeeming our self-confidence and self-esteem is to embrace our purpose and dedicate ourselves to an unfettered pursuit of it.
- If we turn and face the travail, things will be better because we will be better—wiser, seasoned, and more equipped to take on all life has to offer.
- It is not what we learn in times of tribulation that is most important, but rather the person we become, for in the midst of the storm we become the person we need to be to accomplish the purpose for which we were created.
- We have the choice in the process to choose victimization or sovereignty.
- Creating an expectation of fairness in an inherently unfair world can lead to a descent into victimization where one's circumstances are allowed to rule over us.
- Accepting that life is as it is, and dealing with it on that basis is the act of a sovereign who chooses to reign and overcome every obstacle in his way.
- Sovereignty is the sworn enemy of blame, shame, and victimization.
- Personal acts of sovereignty exist on multiple levels and reside in the battlefield of the mind where the fight for our self-image, self-respect, inner health, and sense of accomplishment is waged.
- The core competencies of sovereignty are:
  - Personal Responsibility
  - Independence of thought
  - Emotional health
  - Supremacy over circumstance
  - Ruling by principle
  - Power of the present
- Choosing to live as a sovereign is a cognitive decision that protects inner health and well-being.

- Sovereignty forms a man's core of inner strength and empowers fatherhood.

CHAPTER 8—THE VALUE OF FAILURE

- Failure is not the ultimate defeat, for it is at the point of failure we often find the entry into our destined place of purpose.
- Perfection as a goal is unattainable, and spending ourselves in its pursuit will leave us exhausted and facing the feelings we fear the most.
- Failure is a gift whose value is difficult to measure and nearly impossible to appreciate.
- As humans, we have a tremendous capacity to fail, learn, and then succeed mightily.
- When we embrace the lessons of failure we often find that we are being prepared for the moment of our greatest achievement.
- The failures of our children represent a strategic opportunity for a father to demonstrate his love and to teach the most valuable of life's lessons.
- Failure provides a father an opportunity to demonstrate that his love for his child is totally unconditional.
- The vital role of a father in guiding a child through failure cannot be reliably replicated.
- When a child fails, a father has an important decision to make—is it time to throw a lifeline or is it time to allow them to learn that actions have consequences?
- Every man, regardless of his upbringing, regardless of his shortcomings, and regardless of his life situation, has it in his DNA to be the kind of father that can guide his children.
- The fear of failure, not the failure itself, is what guarantees failure's power over us.
- Love of ourselves is the antidote that thwarts that power.

CHAPTER 9—CULTURE OF HONOR

- The words of fatherhood must infuse the voice of every man of influence if our civilization is to remain healthy and vital.
- Honor is how our founding fathers chose to describe the essence of who they were. It was the one thing they described as sacred.
- Honor is the concept that constitutes the fundamental of understanding what is necessary for men to become men of influence and true fathers.
- Honor is not what a man does but, rather, what he is.
- We are all complex and imperfect beings, yet capable of living lives dedicated to following a path of honor.
- Honor is the essence of who a man is and what drives him.
- Decisions made by honorable men are instinctual, emanating unconsciously from their core values.
- If an honorable man were to lose his honor he would sink into incapacity.

CHAPTER 10—THE FOUNDATIONAL PILLARS OF HONOR

- The foundational pillars of honor are: character, integrity, morality, and competence.
- Character is the measure of the quality of man, i.e. the quality of materials and workmanship by which he is made.
- Good character is formed piece by piece, through hundreds of decisions day by day regarding how we treat our fellow human beings.
- A man of character is a highly principled person with a finely tuned sense of responsibility which governs him.
- Character is formed by the probing questions we ask ourselves, such as:

- Is it the right thing to do?
- What does this say about who I am?
- How does this decision affect the other person?
- What is my responsibility in the matter?
- What is my purpose?
- Integrity is a complex idea composed of truthfulness, honesty, and dependability.
- A man dedicated to a life of integrity is comfortable in his own skin.
- A man of integrity is unwilling to sacrifice that quality for personal gain or comfort.
- Integrity goes much deeper than truth, it defines a man's business relationships and his ethics in the workplace.
- A man of integrity is dependable and can be counted on to fulfill his obligations.
- To a man of integrity, the spirit of agreement is as important as the letter of it.
- Men of integrity can be counted on to do what they said they would do simply because they said they would do it.
- Morality is the systems of rights and wrongs upon which the strength of a civilization depends.
- Morality is the code by which we restrain our inner demons.
- The quality and health of a civilization is dependent upon its moral code.
- The war for the souls of men is waged on the battlefield of morality.
- The moral character of a society is largely defined by its protection of the weak.
- Competence comes in two forms: professional and personal.
- A man of honor will find his place in his profession and take pride in the competence with which he does his work.
- Personal competence speaks directly to a man's ability to successfully navigate through life.

- Personal competence is independent of profession or education, but is derived from his inner strength, judgment, self-control, and wisdom.
- It is the quality of personal competence which is desperately needed to nurture a new generation of fathers.

CHAPTER 11—END OF OUR TALE

- We are in need of competent men to step forward to help heal our land.
- In many ways, we are stranded on the highway of history.
- There are three long-standing problems in this country that need to be addressed: the throw-away people, the tangled web of fault, and sexual abuse.
- Healthy, competent fathers are needed to put a stop to the endless cycle of blame and recrimination.
- Solutions will never be found through a process that labels the other side as evil.
- Diminishing an entire class of people to address the grievances of another class will only ensure that the injustice is never rectified.
- Solutions will not be found by identifying the person responsible for creating a problem and getting them to accept blame for it.
- We are each responsible for our own actions, and the behavior of someone else will not relieve us of that responsibility.
- The only solution lies in taking ownership of the present, forgiving the past, and focusing on solutions for the future.
- Competent fathers are desperately needed to bring wisdom and sound judgment to the process.
- Fathers of integrity are needed in every nook and cranny of this nation.

- This country desperately needs men who will answer the call, who will come, who are prepared, and who will know what to do when they get there.
- Men of honor are needed to empower us all to fulfill our nation's highest purpose.
- Each of us is uniquely qualified and perfectly positioned to positively impact those in our own sphere of influence.
- The solutions to the problems facing us must come from among us.
- If you answer the call and reach out with a hand of friendship and fatherhood, you will see great things happen, and you will experience of the joy of doing something to help one of your fellow travelers along the way.

END NOTES

1. Robert Frost, *The Road not Taken* (Mountain Interval, Holt 1916)

2. Albert Einstein, *Albert Einstein, Historical and Cultural Perspectives (*Princeton NJ, Princeton University Press,1982)

3. *Hidden Figures,* directed by Theodore Melfi. (2016; Los Angeles CA: 20th Century Fox, Film)

4. Vernon Howard, *The Power of Your Supermind,* (New Life Foundation, 2011)

5. Wikipedia contributors, "Columbia Bar" *In Wikipedia, the free encyclopedia.* n.d. Accessed December 24, 2018. https://en.wikipedia.org/wiki/Columbia_Bar.

6. Wikiquote contributors. "William F. Halsey, Jr." In Wikiquotes. Accessed December 24, 2018. https://en.wikiquote.org/wiki/William_Frederick_Halsey,_Jr.

7. Samuel L. Clemens, *Life on the Missisippi* (New York, Harper and Brothers, 1917)

8. Raymond Chandler, *The Simple Act of Murder,* (Houghton Miffin Co, 1950)

9. Doug Johnson and Kim Williams, 2002, Three Wooden Crosses, *Rise and Shine,* Curb Records – WD2-886236, www.discogs.com/Randy-Travis-Rise-And-Shine/release/2921871

10. William B. Travis, *Letter from the Alamo*, February 24, 1836. Texas State Library and Archives Division, Austin Texas.

11. Wikipedia contributors, "1900 Galveston Huricane" *In Wikipedia, the free encyclopedia.* n.d. Accessed December 24, 2018. https://en.wikipedia.org/wiki/1900_Galveston_hurricane.

12. Wikipedia contributors, "Spindletop" *In Wikipedia, the free encyclopedia.* n.d. Accessed December 24, 2018. https://en.wikipedia.org/wiki/Spindletop.

13. Tony Arata, April 30, 1990, The Dance, Garth Brooks, Capitol Records Nashville – 44629,

14. Theodore Roosevelt, "Citizenship in a Republic." The Sorbonne, Paris, France, April 23, 1910.

15. Thomas Jefferson, *Declaration of Independence*, July 4, 1776, Rotunda for the Charters of Freedom, National Archiver Museum, Washington DC.

16. Dr. Martin Luther King, I've Been to the Mountaintop. Bishop Charles Mason Temple, Memphis Tennessee, April 3, 1968.

17. Dietrich Bonhoeffer, https://www.goodreads.com/quotes/82814-there-is-meaning-in-every-journey-that-is-unknown-to

ABOUT THE AUTHOR

Gary D. Rogers grew up in the gulf coast town of Freeport, Texas. The younger of two sons, he was raised by parents who maintained a life-long, loving relationship in a stable middle-class home. From Stephen F. Austin State University he received a BS in biology and chemistry, along with a Masters degree in aquatic ecology. As a young man he lived in the inner city of Brooklyn, New York, where he came face to face with the ravages of poverty, and the crime, drugs, and violence that poverty begets. It was here he began to understand that the problems this country faces will not be fixed by government, that the answers to our most devastating problems must come from the people.

Gary has been blessed with a wonderful family of his own—a loving wife of forty-four years, three great children, and one rather precocious grandson. He has a passion to protect and preserve our culture so that they, and future generations, continue to enjoy the freedoms that our country cherishes. His greatest hope is that all people live life to its fullest and accomplish all that was meant for them to achieve.

By writing this book, Gary seeks to share his own rich life experiences and the lessons he has learned along the way. The blessings of family, the events that shaped his character, and the hard times he has walked through, have all blended to forge a perspective which he presents in these pages, hoping to share valuable life lessons with his readers. His mission is to inspire authenticity in men, to equip both women and men with workable life skills and perspectives, and to empower a healthy culture of fatherhood in our country.